PRESIDENT OBAMA

Other Books by The Poynter Institute

Pope John Paul II: May 18, 1920–April 2, 2005

September 11, 2001: A Collection of Newspaper Front Pages

PRESIDENT OBAMA

Election 2008

A Collection of Newspaper Front Pages
Selected by The Poynter Institute

With an Introduction by
G. B. Trudeau

Andrews McMeel
Publishing, LLC
Kansas City

Paperback edition:

ISBN-13: 978-0-7407-8480-4

ISBN-10: 0-7407-8480-3

Hardcover edition:

ISBN-13: 978-0-7407-8483-5

ISBN-10: 0-7407-8483-8

Library of Congress Control Number is on file.

08 09 10 11 12 RR3 10 9 8 7 6 5 4 3 2 1

www.andrewsmcmeel.com

ATTENTION: SCHOOLS AND BUSINESSES

Andrews McMeel books are available at quantity discounts with bulk purchase for educational, business, or sales promotional use. For information, please write to: Special Sales Department, Andrews McMeel Publishing, 1130 Walnut Street, Kansas City, Missouri 64106.

To all who create change in the face of challenge,
especially journalists who insist on telling the stories democracy demands

CONTENTS

Introduction by G. B. Trudeau xi

U.S. NEWSPAPERS

NATIONAL NEWSPAPERS

INTERNATIONAL NEWSPAPERS

INTRODUCTION

By G. B. Trudeau

In the real world, as a matter of record, there isn't much dancing in the streets. Setting aside sanctioned festivals, it's mostly just a figure of speech, especially when used predictively (see "Iraq, invasion of").

Election Day, November 4, 2008, was different.

That night, Baltimore Avenue in Philadelphia was clogged with a jubilant mob boogying with abandon, banging pots and pans in time with horn blasts from engulfed cars. In Kisumu, thousands of Kenyans shimmied in the streets, singing, kissing, thumping on drums in such an unalloyed outpouring of euphoria that the government was moved to declare a national holiday. In Seattle, a club turned its speakers into the street, blasting a beat for the enormous dance party that rocked downtown. In Jakarta, schoolchildren hugged and danced in the pouring rain. In New Haven, hundreds of Yale students, mad with joy, spontaneously poured from their rooms and converged on a campus green, where they formed an enormous circle of celebration. And in Manhattan, Broadway was quickly cordoned off as thousands of New Yorkers streamed south toward the lights, dancing, shouting, overcome by a big, bold blast of history, the kind that filled up Times Square on V-J Day.

And then the next day, after the street parties were over, people went out and did something many of them hadn't done in years: They bought newspapers.

Yes, newspapers.

By the trainload, actually. *The Washington Post* printed up 30,000 extra copies; they sold out instantly. So they ordered 250,000 copies of a commemorative edition, then printed another 350,000, eventually totaling 900,000—offered at triple the usual cover price. In Los Angeles, the *Times* printed up an extra 107,000, but they were gone in an instant, so outside their downtown offices, a line of customers formed around the block. Two days later it was still there. The paper eventually sold more than 300,000 extra copies. Meanwhile, *The New York Times* put an extra 250,000 papers on the street, but individual copies still popped up on eBay for $200 apiece. And at last count, *USA Today* had printed about 430,000 additional copies, with online sales still brisk.

All those folks scrambling for copies weren't just interested in election returns, obviously. They could, after all, get the details from TV or the Internet, and probably already had—maybe even from their local newspaper's Web site. But what they couldn't get was the crisp, tactile, iconic artifact that is a daily newspaper—that tangible proof that something big had really happened. The morning-after newspaper, with the huge headlines reserved for historic events, continues to be seen as the indispensable keepsake—one that can forever evoke and refresh a deeply consequential memory.

To our industry, it was a glorious day and no doubt will be recalled fondly. It seems doubtful, with newspapers inexorably losing their place in public life, that we will see many more like it. But on November 5, 2008, for one day, we became a nation of newspaper consumers again. Across the country, editors were breaking out the 72-point type, and the public couldn't get enough of it.

This collection of front pages evolved from that continuing excitement, and part of its great appeal is that it allows readers to vicariously experience the same ringing event from many vantage points. Each newspaper had its own particular cultural or geographic perspective, so while the basic lead ("Obama wins!") was the same everywhere, there was considerable variation in the framing. For Hawaiian readers, for instance, it was a hometown-boy-makes-good story. For Atlanta, with its civil rights legacy, the story is the ultimate triumph of social justice. In *The Arizona Republic*, John McCain's home newspaper, the smiling winner shares the front page with a gracious loser.

To look at these disparate front pages in sequence is to grasp the enormity of Barack Obama's dream of bringing a fractious country together. But the overriding tone of elation and pride suggests he's off to a pretty good start.

Did I mention there was dancing in the streets?

G. B. Trudeau is the creator of Doonesbury.

ELECTION 2008   8 PAGES OF COVERAGE INSIDE

The Birmingham News

al www.al.com EM123   *Wednesday, November 5, 2008* ♦ *Our 121st year*   30¢ home delivery ♦ 75¢ newsstand

OBAMA WINS

PRESIDENT-ELECT | 'Change has come to America'
CONGRESS | Democrats expand control of Senate and House. **4B-5B**

AP/MORRY GASH

"If there is anyone out there who still doubts that America is a place where all things are possible; who still wonders if the dream of our founders is alive in our time; who still questions the power of our democracy, tonight is your answer," president-elect Barack Obama said during his acceptance speech in Chicago on Tuesday.

1

In the Deep South, where a Democratic presidential candidate hasn't won since Jimmy Carter, the "civil rights legacy" was given special attention.

THE ALABAMA VOTE

More than 2 million Alabamians cast ballots

By CHARLES J. DEAN
News staff writer

Record numbers of Alabama voters kept the state Republican red Tuesday, but it mattered little on a day that saw Democratic Sen. Barack Obama defeat Sen. John McCain to become the nation's first African-American president.

"It's a wonderful piece of history, a wonderful time in history, almost a miraculous time, from my point of

view," said Richard Arrington as, at his home, he watched television networks declare Obama the winner; he will be the nation's 44th president. Arrington knows a little something about making history: He was elected Birmingham's first black mayor 29 years ago.

At the Bottle Tree Cafe, on Birmingham's Southside, a crowd of about 200 Obama

See ALABAMA | Page 3B

THE CIVIL RIGHTS LEGACY

Civil rights foot soldiers watch a racial sea change

**By TOM GORDON,
THOMAS SPENCER
and GREG GARRISON**
News staff writers

Even as they made history, breaking down barriers to black participation in American life, Fred Gray, Richard Arrington and Alvin Holmes never believed they would live long enough to see a black man elected president.

All were happy to be proved wrong by Barack Obama on Tuesday night.

"It tells me the country is headed in the right direction because in order for him to be where he is now, he had to receive a lot of votes from people who do not look like he does," said Gray, who represented civil rights figures such as Rosa Parks and

See CIVIL | Page 2B

STATES WON

OBAMA McCAIN Not called

Unofficial results as of 1 a.m. CST

Electoral vote

OBAMA **338**   McCAIN **159**

Not called **40**

Popular vote

55,942,990   51,030,831
OBAMA **52% 47%** McCAIN

Others 1,336,306 — 1%

ALABAMA RESULTS 97% of precincts reporting

JOHN McCAIN
1,217,628 votes
60%

BARACK OBAMA
788,141 votes
39%

INSIDE

How will Obama lead? 1B

Alabama Supreme Court race undecided. 1B

In exit polls, women, blacks support Obama. 8B

THE PRESIDENTIAL RACE

Nation elects its first black president

By DAVID ESPO
The Associated Press

WASHINGTON

Barack Obama swept to victory as the nation's first black president Tuesday night in an electoral college landslide that overcame racial barriers as old as America itself. "Change has come to America," he told a jubilant hometown Chicago crowd estimated at nearly a quarter-million people.

The son of a black father from Kenya and a white mother from Kansas, the Democratic senator from Illinois sealed his historic triumph by defeating Republican Sen. John McCain in a string of wins in hard-fought battleground states — Ohio, Florida, Iowa and more. He captured Virginia, too, the first candidate of his party in 44 years to do so.

On a night for Democrats to savor, they not only elected Obama the nation's 44th president but padded their majorities in the House and Senate, and in January will control both the White House and Congress for the first time since 1994.

See PRESIDENT | Page 3B

WEATHER
Details / **6C**

High **78**   Low **51**

IN TODAY'S PAPER
An interview with John Parker Wilson
SPORTS | Section D

For home delivery, call **205-325-4444**

Printed on 100% recycled paper

50 cents

ELECTION2008

Final Edition

Anchorage Daily News

Wednesday, November 5, 2008 | BREAKING NEWS AT ADN.COM | Alaska's Newspaper

U.S. SENATE
Stevens leads tight race
Found guilty of seven felony counts last month, Sen. Ted Stevens was leading challenger Mark Begich.

○ Begich, Mark (D)   46.46%
○ Stevens, Ted (R)   48.12%

96% of precincts reporting
Story, Page A-9

ADN.COM
Go online for the latest results, videos and more photos from election night and to join the conversation on the Alaska Politics blog.

U.S. HOUSE
Young holds solid advantage
Despite polls that predicted a defeat, Rep. Don Young was ahead of challenger Ethan Berkowitz.

○ Berkowitz, Ethan (D) 43.89%
○ Young, Don (R)   51.55%

96% of precincts reporting
Story, Page A-10

Obama makes history

President-elect Barack Obama acknowledges a cheering crowd at an election night party in Chicago's Grant Park on Tuesday. Obama won the electoral vote by more than a 2-to-1 margin.

MORRY GASH / The Associated Press

Illinois senator is elected nation's first black president

By STEVEN THOMMA | McClatchy Newspapers

WASHINGTON — Barack Obama was elected the 44th president of the United States on Tuesday, swept to victory by a country eager to change course at home and abroad. Obama, 47, becomes the first African-American in U.S. history to win the presidency and the first from the generation that came of age after the turbulence of the 1960s.

See Page A-6, OBAMA

Winner by state

■ Obama   ■ McCain
     Not called

■ R.I.
■ Del.
■ D.C.

Unofficial results as of 10:13 p.m. AST

Electoral votes   270 needed to win

Obama   349
McCain   145

The Associated Press

Gov. Sarah Palin is joined by her husband, Todd, at a Phoenix rally where Sen. John McCain made his concession speech Tuesday evening. The McCain-Palin ticket was a big winner in Alaska.

ELISE AMENDOLA / The Associated Press

Inside

 PRESIDENTIAL ELECTION
PAGE A-6 & A-7

GOV. SARAH PALIN
PAGE A-8

ALASKA LEGISLATURE
PAGE A-11

 VOTE RESULTS
PAGE A-11

2

Way up north, vice presidential nominee and governor Sarah Palin was a key face of election night.

ARPAIO, THOMAS CRUISE TO WINS AA12
DEMS CONTROL ARIZONA'S U.S. HOUSE DELEGATION AA14

THE ARIZONA REPUBLIC
SPECIAL ELECTION EDITION
50¢ | azcentral.com | WEDNESDAY, NOVEMBER 5, 2008

OBAMA SEIZES HISTORIC WIN

Dominance in swing states leads to decisive victory

Arizonan McCain gracious in defeat, calls for unity

PABLO MARTINEZ MONSIVAIS/ASSOCIATED PRESS

Before a crowd of more than 100,000 in Chicago's Grant Park, President-elect Barack Obama took the stage to declare a "defining moment" in American politics.

20-PAGE SPECIAL SECTION

ACROSS THE NATION

Congressional gains
Democrats pick up at least five Senate seats in Congress but look likely to fall short of a filibuster-proof majority. The party is expected to pick up 20 House seats. **AA6**

Revolutionary victory
Barack Obama wins at least seven states carried by President Bush in the previous election, making good on his promise to redraw the electoral map. An analyst calls his triumph "truly revolutionary." **AA5**

IN ARIZONA

GOP retains Legislature
Republicans appear to keep their hold on the state Legislature. **AA14**

School mergers fail
Voters pass only one of six plans to unify school districts. **AA16**

PROPOSITIONS
100: REAL-ESTATE TAX BAN . . . **YES**
102: GAY-MARRIAGE BAN . . . . **YES**
202: HIRING SANCTIONS . . . . . . **NO**
All proposition results, AA15

ROB SCHUMACHER/THE ARIZONA REPUBLIC

John McCain, with wife Cindy and supporters at the Arizona Biltmore Resort in Phoenix, accepted defeat and noted "the special significance" of Obama's win.

U.S. POPULAR VOTE
With 85 percent of precincts reporting

52% | **47%**
OBAMA | McCAIN

ELECTORAL VOTE *(270 needed to win)*
Tally does not include Mo., Mont., N.C.

349 | **159**
OBAMA | McCAIN

Obama shatters barrier to become 1st Black president

By Dan Nowicki
THE ARIZONA REPUBLIC

Barack Obama, the cool and collected Hawaiian-born son of a man from Kenya and woman from Kansas, whose promise of "change" inspired a generation of young people, shattered the last racial ceiling in U.S. politics Tuesday to become the first African-American elected president.

Obama, a freshman Democratic senator from Illinois, crushed his Republican foe, Sen. John McCain of Arizona, to capture a White House controlled for the past eight years by GOP President George W. Bush. In a striking repudiation of the Bush era, Obama won in an Electoral College landslide.

Obama's historic win comes 40 years after the assassination of civil-rights icon Martin Luther King Jr. and 45 years after King's dramatic "I Have a Dream" speech. And it comes at a time when the United States is militarily engaged in Iraq and Afghanistan and reeling under economic pressures not felt in decades.

"It's been a long time coming, but tonight, because of what we did on this

See **OBAMA** Page AA2

GET THE LATEST UPDATES, BLOGS, SLIDE SHOWS AND MORE AT
ELECTIONS.AZCENTRAL.COM

THE ARIZONA REPUBLIC

Cities balking at crime lab fees

Your daily 'Republic' inside: A second mistrial ends the murder case against an Arizona border agent. Find this story inside, along with Valley & State, Sports and Food & Drink.

A Gannett Newspaper
119th year, No. 171. Copyright
2008, The Arizona Republic

3

In Senator John McCain's home state, which he won by nine percentage points, his concession speech was captured on the front page.

WEDNESDAY, NOVEMBER 5, 2008

Los Angeles Times

50¢ DESIGNATED AREAS HIGHER © 2008   82 PAGES   latimes.com

IT'S OBAMA

DECISIVE VICTORY MAKES HISTORY

In California, gay-marriage ban takes early lead

4

As the Times *declared "a smashing electoral college victory" for Senator Barack Obama, it also reported that the state was poised to pass a ban on gay marriage, which had been legal there for only six months.*

TANNEN MAURY European Pressphoto Agency

'CHANGE HAS COME': President-elect Barack Obama celebrates with his wife, Michelle, their daughters, Sasha and Malia, and more than 240,000 supporters gathered along Chicago's waterfront. Many wept at the landmark moment.

The first black president-elect wins a solid mandate and a fortified Democratic majority in Congress.

MARK Z. BARABAK

Barack Obama, the son of a father from Kenya and a white mother from Kansas, was elected the nation's 44th president Tuesday, breaking the ultimate racial barrier to become the first African American to claim the country's highest office.

A nation founded by slave owners and seared by civil war and generations of racial strife delivered a smashing electoral college victory to the 47-year-old first-term senator from Illinois, who forged a broad, multiracial, multiethnic coalition. His victory was a leap in the march toward equality: When Obama was born, people with his skin color could not even vote in parts of America, and many were killed for trying.

"If there is anyone out there who still doubts that America is a place where all things are possible, who still wonders if the dream of our founders is alive in our time, who still questions the power of our democracy, tonight is your answer," Obama told more than 240,000 celebrants gathered along Chicago's waterfront. Many had tears streaking their faces.

"It's been a long time coming," said Obama, who strode on stage with his wife, Michelle, and their two daughters, Sasha and Malia. "But tonight, because of what we did on this day, in this election, at this defining moment, change has come to America."

Obama was beating Republican John McCain in every state Democrats carried four years ago, including Pennsylvania, which McCain had worked vigorously to pry away. Obama also made significant inroads into Republican turf, carrying Ohio, Colorado and Virginia; the latter voted Democratic for the first time in more than 40 years. He won the swing states of Florida, New Hampshire, Iowa and New Mexico, which backed President Bush in 2004.

In winning the White House, Obama to a large degree remade the electorate: About 1 in 10 of those casting ballots Tuesday were doing so for the first time. Though that number

[See **Election,** Page A8]

MATTHEW CAVANAUGH EPA
"Whatever our differences, we are fellow Americans," John McCain conceded.

NEWS ANALYSIS

Now it's idealism versus realism

DOYLE McMANUS
REPORTING FROM WASHINGTON

Barack Obama won the presidency Tuesday by persuading voters to embrace a seeming paradox: leadership based on contradictory principles of change and reassurance.

The Illinois senator combined ambitious goals and a cautious temperament. He promised tax cuts, better healthcare, new energy programs and fiscal discipline all at the same time, and all without the bitterness and stalemate that arose when those issues were tackled in the past.

Now, as Obama moves through his transition to the White House, this effort to square the political circle becomes the defining challenge in the months ahead. Which Barack Obama will dominate as he begins to govern?

Too much of the ambitious

[See **Analysis,** Page A11]

Nation watches as state weighs ban

Prop. 8 battle drew money and attention from across the U.S.

JESSICA GARRISON,
CARA MIA DiMASSA
AND RICHARD PADDOCK

A measure to ban gay marriage in California led in early returns Tuesday although the final outcome remained in doubt, leaving advocates on both sides in suspense about the most divisive and emotionally fraught contest in the state this year.

Proposition 8 would amend the California Constitution to define marriage as being only between a man and a woman.

Proposition 8 was the most expensive proposition on any ballot in the nation this year, with more than $74 million spent by both sides.

The measure's most fervent

proponents believed that nothing less than the future of traditional families was at stake, while opponents believed that they were fighting for the fundamental right of gay people to be treated equally under the law.

In San Francisco, supporters of gay marriage packed a ballroom at the Westin St. Francis Hotel on Tuesday night.

"You decided to live your life out loud. You fell in love and you said 'I do.' Tonight, we await a verdict," San Francisco Mayor Gavin Newsom said to a

[See **Prop. 8,** Page A21]

PROPOSITION 8
Eliminate gay marriage

YES	NO
52.5%	47.5%

Results as of 11:33 p.m. Pacific time with 48% of precincts reporting

ELECTORAL VOTES
270 needed to win

OBAMA	McCAIN	UNDECIDED
349	144	45

111TH CONGRESS
The House of Representatives
218 seats to control the House

DEMOCRATS	REPUBLICANS	UNDECIDED
242	160	33

The Senate
51 seats to control the Senate

DEMOCRATS	REPUBLICANS	UNDECIDED
56*	40	4

* Includes 2 independents. All results as of 11:10 p.m. Pacific time

Analysis: Erasing race assumptions
Even in Virginia, heart of the Confederacy, Obama prevails. **A11**

They wouldn't miss this for the world
Voters turn out in droves to take their part in history. **A15**

Roundup of state propositions
Measures on redistricting and farm animals are ahead. **A20**

latimes.com

All the latest news
View interactive maps detailing results for elections around the country and for all statewide measures and propositions.

Where hope has wrestled with fear

SANDY BANKS
REPORTING FROM CLEVELAND

I could not have imagined that less than four years later, he would be elected president.

His name was so unfamiliar, I kept stumbling over it during our 45-minute interview about the role of race in his life and in his politics. Was it Barack Obama or Obama Barack?

The next morning, unbidden, he called me back.

"Hey Sandy," he said. "This is Barack. I've been thinking about what we talked about, and I wanted to add some thoughts."

By the time we finished our second chat, there were two things I thought I knew:

Barack Obama was determined to force this country to confront its "legacy of slavery."

And what he was asking — and offering — was too much for a nation still bitterly divided by skin color.

"His candidacy would make this country squirm and shudder and maybe even come unglued," I wrote back then.

Clearly, I underestimated him — and us.

How could I have been so wrong? Last week, as Obama closed in on the presidency, I went back to my hometown to look for answers.

Cleveland was a step up for my parents. My father's family fled Georgia in the 1920s, one step ahead of a lynch mob set on teaching my uncle a lesson for daring to sass a white man. Twenty years later, my mother led her siblings north from a farm in Alabama. She met my father in Cleveland. They married, and I was the oldest

[See **Banks,** Page A12]

Weather Page B10
Complete Index........A2

TODAY'S INSIDE SECTIONS
California, Business,
Sports, Calendar and Food

Printed with soy inks on
partially recycled paper.

7 85944 00050 6

ELECTION 2008: COVERAGE BEGINS ON PAGE A3

San Francisco Chronicle

I Voted!
我已投票!
¡Ya Voté!

★★★★★ Z 1 3 5 6 | Printed on recycled paper | **WEDNESDAY, NOVEMBER 5, 2008** | sfgate.com | 415-777-1111 75¢

OBAMA
"CHANGE HAS COME TO AMERICA"

PRESIDENT-ELECT BARACK OBAMA *in his victory speech in Chicago*

YOUR PHOTOS
Send us your shots from election-night parties. *sfgate.com/ZFGQ*

ASIAN POP
Common ground between Asian Americans, gays. *sfgate.com/ZFHN*

WEATHER
Partly cloudy.
Highs 56 to 65.
Lows 43 to 54. **C6**
Index is on Page A2

7 38805 10005 1

5

Below the newspaper's name appears an "I voted" emblem—in English, Chinese, and Spanish—just like the stickers voters received as they left the polls.

ELECTION 2008 8 PAGES OF COVERAGE INSIDE
MORE AT SANLUISOBISPO.COM

Newspaper of the Central Coast • SanLuisObispo.com

THE TRIBUNE

FOR HOME DELIVERY: 800-288-4128 — SAN LUIS OBISPO COUNTY, CALIFORNIA — WEDNESDAY, NOVEMBER 5, 2008 — 50¢

FULL LOCAL RESULTS A6-9

SHIELD INITIATIVE REJECTED A6

GROWTH WINS IN ATASCADERO

Shield opponents Clay, Fonzi and **Kelley** win seats on council

SLO COUNTY MAYOR & COUNCIL RACES
ROMERO HEADS NEW SLO COUNCIL A7
PETERS LEADS IN MORRO BAY A8
REISS GETS NEW TERM IN PISMO A7
EASY WIN FOR **SHOALS** IN GROVER A7
PASO'S MAYOR RACE UNDECIDED A6

PROPOSITION 8 A4
CLOSE FIGHT OVER GAY MARRIAGE
Narrow lead for 'Yes on 8'

OBAMA **338** McCAIN **145**: OBAMA WINS ON WAVE OF CHANGE
ELECTORAL COLLEGE TOTALS AS OF 12 A.M.

AMERICAN HISTORY

President-elect Barack Obama, left, his wife Michelle Obama, right, and two daughters, Sasha and Malia, salute the crowd at Tuesday's election night celebration in Chicago.

LANDMARK DAY DELIVERS A DECISIVE VICTORY TO BARACK OBAMA, AMERICA'S FIRST BLACK PRESIDENT

MORE PRESIDENTIAL COVERAGE INSIDE
HOW AMERICA VOTED: A graphic look at the numbers behind Tuesday's election. **A12**
WHAT'S NEXT? After historic win, Obama now faces a range of difficult problems. **A3**
LOCAL REACTION: African-American family from Arroyo Grande celebrates historic day. **A3**

By ADAM NAGOURNEY
New York Times

Barack Hussein Obama was elected the 44th president of the United States on Tuesday, sweeping away the last racial barrier in American politics with ease as the country chose him as its first black chief executive.

The election of Obama amounted to a national catharsis — a repudiation of a historically unpopular Republican president and his economic and foreign policies, and an embrace of Obama's call for a change in the direction and the tone of the country.

But it was just as much a strikingly symbolic moment in the evolution of the nation's fraught racial history, a breakthrough that would have seemed unthinkable just two years ago.

Obama, 47, a first-term senator from Illinois, defeated Sen. John McCain of Arizona, 72, a former prisoner of war who was making his second bid for the presidency. To the very end, McCain's campaign was eclipsed by an opponent who was nothing short of a phenomenon, drawing huge crowds epitomized by the tens of thousands of people who turned out Tuesday night to hear Obama's victory speech in Grant Park in Chicago.

McCain also fought the headwinds of a relentlessly

Please see PRESIDENT, Back Page

DEMOCRATS STRENGTHEN HOLD ON CONGRESS A5

CAPPS SECURES A SEVENTH TERM A9 | **MALDONADO** CRUISES TO EASY WIN A9 | **BLAKESLEE** TOPS CUTHBERT AGAIN A9

INSIDE TODAY
Business B6, Classifieds E1, Comics S4, Crossword F7, Dear Abby S5, Horoscope S5, Lottery A2, Movies B3, Obituaries B2, Opinion B4, Stocks B7, Television S5

INDUSTRIAL EXPLOSION KILLS PASO MAN B1

DINNER-AND-A-MOVIE HAS NEW MEANING B6

Rocky Mountain News

OBAMA

Colorado key in electing first black president

Udall win boosts Dems' margin in U.S. Senate

7

This daily in Denver, where Obama accepted the Democratic nomination for president, trumpeted Colorado's first blue-state vote since 1992.

8

The Courant *chose a bold approach: a horizontal photo taking up the entire front page. "We felt something simple with a single quote delivered a powerful statement," said design director Melanie Shaffer.*

"At this defining moment, change has come to America." — **President-elect Barack Oba**

9

aking to the crowd at Chicago's Grant Park shortly after midnight this morning

THE OLDEST COLLEGE DAILY · FOUNDED 1878

Yale Daily News

NEW HAVEN, CONNECTICUT · **WEDNESDAY, NOVEMBER 5, 2008** · VOL. CXXXI, NO. 47 · yaledailynews.com

'THIS IS OUR MOMENT'

BARACK OBAMA, 44TH PRESIDENT, PROMISES CHANGE

10

This is the first election since 1968 that has not had a Yale alumnus on the Republican or Democratic presidential ticket.

CHRIS MCGRATH/GETTY IMAGES

IN VICTORY SPEECH, ILLINOIS SENATOR PROCLAIMS 'A NEW DAWN' FOR THE UNITED STATES AND PLEDGES TO WORK TOWARD PROSPERITY, PEACE AND THE AMERICAN DREAM

BY ISAAC ARNSDORF and MARTINE POWERS
STAFF REPORTERS

CHICAGO — Sen. Barack Obama shattered racial barriers and ushered in a new era of American politics on Tuesday by decisively defeating his Republican rival to become the 44th president of the United States of America.

Obama, the 47-year-old son of a Kansan mother and a Kenyan father, topped Sen. John McCain of Arizona to conclude the longest, most expensive campaign in the country's history. The sentiment in Chicago's Grant Park, where Obama declared victory, was clear: America had gotten its money's worth.

To become the nation's first black president-elect, the Illinois senator banded together a coalition augmented by minorities and young people who embraced his message of change and repudiated the past eight years of Republican rule under President George W. Bush '68.

"This victory alone is not the change we seek," Obama said in his acceptance speech here. "It is only the chance for us to make that change."

Vote-counting continued in the early hours of Wednesday morning, but with more than three-quarters of precincts reporting as of 4:30 a.m., Obama had amassed 52 percent of the popular vote to McCain's 47 percent. In the electoral college, CNN projected an Obama lead of 338 to 163, with votes in Missouri, Indiana and North Carolina yet to be assigned.

A redefined electoral map lifted Obama above the 270 electoral votes required to win. Obama won every state Sen. John Kerry '66 picked up in 2004 while also turning states formerly loyal to President George W. Bush '68, such as Florida and Virginia.

Though the campaign was cautious about declaring victory too early Tuesday, the 240,000 supporters massing in Chicago's Grant Park began celebrating

SEE **OBAMA** PAGE B4

> America, I have never been more hopeful than I am tonight that we will get there. I promise you, we as a people will get there.
>
> BARACK OBAMA
> President-elect, United States

At McCain camp, the maverick concedes

BY PAUL NEEDHAM
STAFF REPORTER

PHOENIX — One woman stood out at a rally for supporters of Sen. John McCain here last night.

She wore a dress made of plastic McCain yard signs, kept together with duct tape — and nothing else. The woman said she was from Arizona, adding, as she entered the party, that it was the "same state as our next president."

The woman's name was Linda Miracle, and while her dress won her countless admirers at the Arizona Biltmore Resort & Spa, there was no miracle for McCain yesterday.

Instead, McCain lost by a significant margin to Sen. Barack Obama, the Democratic senator from Illinois. He conceded the presidential race here in Phoenix, congratulating Obama and thanking his supporters.

"Senator Obama and I have had and argued on differences, and he has prevailed," McCain said. "I urge all Americans who supported me to join me in not just congratulating him, but also in offering our next president our goodwill and earnest effort to find ways to come together."

McCain's supporters were devastated as vote tallies came in from swing states such

SEE **MCCAIN** PAGE B8

With cries of 'Yes, we did,' Elis celebrate Obama's victory

DANIEL CARVALHO/STAFF PHOTOGRAPHER

BY LAWRENCE GIPSON and DIVYA SUBRAHMANYAM
STAFF REPORTERS

At 12:30 a.m. on Wednesday, Nov. 5, Yale exploded. For the second time.

It started at 211 Park St. A mass of about 100 students that surged towards Old Campus, chanting. "Obama!"

Students rushed out from all corners of campus, in a clear demonstration of their political leanings. (4 in 5 students polled by the News last week said they were voting for the Illinois Senator.)

They charged between Jonathan Edwards and Branford colleges and out into Old Campus to join hands and form a massive circle that stretched from Lanman-Wright Hall to Lawrance Hall, all the way across to Connecticut Hall. Students ran along the inside of the circle as they belted out the national anthem. As the final words sounded into the night, the crowd erupted in cheers, the circle broke and students charged toward the center.

There was kissing and hugging. Students were lifted on shoulders above the crowd, which had become roughly 700-strong.

It was a celebration: Barack Obama had been named president-elect.

SEE **REACTION** PAGE B6

INSIDE THE NEWS

MORNING SHOWERS 62
EVENING SHOWERS 52

VOTE

SPECIAL ISSUE
ELECTION 2008
SECTION B

MARKELL TROUNCES LEE

State Treasurer Jack Markell, a Democrat, rode the promise of change to beat Republican Bill Lee in Delaware's gubernatorial election. Democrats also invoked that theme to win both chambers of the Legislature. **PAGES A10-11**

Among GOP fallen: Spence, Wagner, Valihura, Stone, Lofink. PAGE A11

The News Journal

www.delawareonline.com

WEDNESDAY Nov. 5, 2008 75¢ FINAL EDITION

'YES, WE CAN'

OBAMA ELECTED FIRST BLACK PRESIDENT

BIDEN ACHIEVES HIGHEST OFFICE FOR A DELAWAREAN

"The road ahead will be long. Our climb will be steep. We may not get there in one year or even one term, but America, I have never been more hopeful than I am tonight that we will get there. I promise you — we as a people will get there."

Barack Obama

Barack Obama and Joe Biden acknowledge the cheers of supporters at their victory rally Tuesday night in Chicago.
The News Journal/SUCHAT PEDERSON

COMPLETE RESULTS ★ MORE PHOTOS ★ VIDEO ★ FORUMS GO TO WWW.DELAWAREONLINE.COM

NEW CASTLE, KENT AND SUSSEX COUNTIES AND WILMINGTON RESULTS, PAGE B1

| Once unthinkable, black Delawareans fulfill dream. **PAGE A4** | VP-elect Biden breaks new ground for Delaware. **PAGE A6** | Redemption for Biden after crushing loss in Iowa. **PAGE A7** | Long lines, good feelings at polling stations. **PAGE B1** |

©2008, The News Journal Co
A Gannett newspaper   130th year, No. 161

TODAY'S FORECAST
HIGH LOW
61   49
WILMINGTON
Details on A4

INDEX

Business	B6	Dear Abby	E4	Movies	E4	Scoreboard	C5
Classified	D1	Editorial	A20	Obituaries	B2	Sports	C1
Comics	E5	Letters	A20	People	A4	Stocks	B8
Crossword	E4	Lotteries	B2	Police report	B2	TV listings	E2

INSIDE

Former Boscov's execs to buy chain

Retailer hopes to recover under two of its former leaders after rejecting $11 million buyout offer. **PAGE B6**

Making a difference in our community.
Nominate your hero today. delawareonline.com/jeffersonawards

The News Journal
Worth every minute
www.delawareonline.com

11

In the state Joe Biden represented in the Senate for more than thirty-five years, his front-page image and smile were incandescent.

ELECTION FINAL

22-PAGE SPECIAL SECTION » A25-46

Weather
Today: Rain. High 64.
Low 51.
Thursday: Mostly cloudy.
Low 63. High 52.
Details, B6

The Washington Post

131ST YEAR No. 336   S DM VA K   Printed using recycled fiber
WEDNESDAY, NOVEMBER 5, 2008
Mr Mo Mr Vi Vy Vy Vy Vs
NEWSSTAND 50¢
HOME DELIVERY 41¢

12

As the hometown paper of the nation's capital, where three-quarters of registered voters are Democrats, the Post *sold out by 8 A.M. on November 5. The paper printed an additional 900,000 copies to meet demand.*

Obama Makes History

U.S. DECISIVELY ELECTS FIRST BLACK PRESIDENT

DEMOCRATS EXPAND CONTROL OF CONGRESS

President-elect Barack Obama, with wife Michelle and daughters Sasha, 7, and Malia, 10, greets more than 100,000 people celebrating his victory in Grant Park, in his home town of Chicago.   BY NIKKI KAHN — THE WASHINGTON POST

By ROBERT BARNES
and MICHAEL D. SHEAR
Washington Post Staff Writers

Sen. Barack Obama of Illinois was elected the nation's 44th president yesterday, riding a reformist message of change and an inspirational exhortation of hope to become the first African American to ascend to the White House.

Obama, 47, the son of a Kenyan father and a white mother from Kansas, led a tide of Democratic victories across the nation in defeating Republican Sen. John McCain of Arizona, a 26-year veteran of Washington who could not overcome his connections to President Bush's increasingly unpopular administration.

Standing before a crowd of more than 100,000 who had waited for hours at Chicago's Grant Park, Obama acknowledged his own accomplishment and the dreams of his supporters.

"If there is anyone out there who still doubts that America is a place where all things are possible, who still wonders if the dream of our founders is alive in our time, who still questions the power of our democracy, tonight is your answer," he said just before midnight Eastern time.

"The road ahead will be long. Our climb will be steep. We may not get there in one year or even one term, but America — I have never been more hopeful than I am tonight that we will get there. I promise you — we as a people will get there."

The historic Election Day brought millions of new voters, long lines at polling places nationwide and a new era of Democratic dominance in Congress, even though the party fell short of the 60 votes needed for a veto-proof majority in the Senate. In the House, Democrats made major gains, adding to their already sizable advantage and returning them to a position of power that predates the 1994 Republican revolution.

Democrats will use their new legislative muscle to advance an economic and foreign policy agenda that Bush has largely blocked for eight years. Even when the party seized

See ELECTION, A38, Col. 1

HOW HE WON

Measured Response To Financial Crisis Sealed the Election

By ANNE E. KORNBLUT
Washington Post Staff Writer

Sen. Barack Obama, so steady in public, did not hide his vexation when he summoned his top advisers to meet with him in Chicago on Sept. 14.

His general-election campaign had gone stale. For weeks, he had watched Sen. John McCain suction up the oxygen in the race, driving the news coverage after the boisterous Republican convention in St. Paul, Minn., and suddenly drawing huge crowds with his new running mate, Alaska Gov. Sarah Palin.

Convening the meeting that Sunday in the office of David Axelrod, his chief strategist, Obama was blunt: It was time to get serious.

"He said, 'You know, maybe we can just win it on the issues. But I don't think so,' " recalled senior adviser Anita Dunn. With the debates approaching and just seven weeks until the election, "his charge to everybody was 'Guys, we're back in combat mode,' " Dunn said.

And then, the next morning, a global earthquake hit: Lehman Brothers, the giant investment firm, filed for bankruptcy, triggering the biggest corporate collapse in U.S. history and an international financial meltdown, and transforming the presidential race.

It was a moment neither the senator from Illinois nor his advisers had anticipated, but one for which they were uniquely prepared. In the days that followed, the newly chastised Obama team became more aggressive, with a message they had refined over the summer. The candidate himself, criticized as too cool, too cerebral and too detached, suddenly had the opportunity to show those qualities to be reassuring and presidential.

For McCain, already struggling with the economic

See OBAMA, A34, Col. 1

At an election party at Busboys and Poets, Tiffany Payton and Barbara Mack, right, embrace as CNN declares Obama the winner.   BY BILL O'LEARY — THE WASHINGTON POST

A DAY OF TRANSFORMATION

America's History Gives Way to Its Future

By KEVIN MERIDA
Washington Post Staff Writer

After a day of runaway lines that circled blocks, of ladies hobbling on canes and drummers rollicking on street corners, the enormous significance of Barack Obama's election finally began to sink into the landscape. The magnitude of his win suggested that the country itself might be in a gravitational pull toward a rebirth that some were slow to recognize.

Tears flowed, not only for Obama's historic achievement, but because many were happily discovering that perhaps they had underestimated possibility in America.

When the novelist Kim McLarin watched her vote being recorded at her polling station in Milton, Mass., she stood still for a moment with her 8-year-old son, Isaac. "My heart was full. I could scarcely breathe," she said. "What I've been

forced to acknowledge is there has been a shift — it's not a sea change. But there's been a decided shift in the meaning of race. It's not an ending. It's a beginning."

What kind of beginning it is, Americans were wrestling with late into the night, some popping champagne and others burdened with unease. Would enduring strains of intolerance lose their power or gain rebellious steam? Could new hope be harnessed to create new solutions? Is America ready to pull itself together or resigned to live divided? The campaign that began for Obama 21 months ago had raised in stark terms whether America was ready for a black president. Last night's answer — a resounding yes — raises the next question: How much more change will America embrace?

When McLarin learned last night that the nation had voted

See TRANSFORMATION, A33, Col. 1

THE AGENDA

Hard Choices And Challenges Follow Triumph

By DAN BALZ
Washington Post Staff Writer

After a victory of historic significance, Barack Obama will inherit problems of historic proportions. Not since Franklin D. Roosevelt was inaugurated at the depths of the Great Depression in 1933 has a new president been confronted with the challenges Obama will face as he starts his presidency.

At home, Obama must revive an economy experiencing some of the worst shocks in more than half a century. Abroad, he has pledged to end the war in Iraq and defeat al-Qaeda and the Taliban in Afghanistan. He ran on a platform to change the country and its politics. Now he must begin to spell out exactly how.

Obama's winning percentage appears likely to be the largest of any Democrat since Lyndon Johnson's 1964 landslide and makes him the first since Jimmy Carter in 1976 to garner more than 50.1 percent. Like Johnson, he will govern with sizable congressional majorities. Democrats gained at least five seats in the Senate and looked to add significantly to their strength in the House.

But with those advantages come hard choices. Among them will be deciding how much he owes his victory to a popular rejection of President Bush and the Republicans and how much it represents an embrace of Democratic governance. Interpreting his mandate will be only one of several critical decisions Obama must make as he prepares

See AGENDA, A30, Col. 1

IT'S NOT OVER TILL THE ELECTORAL COLLEGE VOTES B6

Florida COURIER

Sharing Black Life, Statewide

PRESORTED STANDARD MAIL U.S. POSTAGE PAID DAYTONA BEACH, FL PERMIT #189

I VOTED

FREE

VOLUME 16 NO. 45S   NOVEMBER 7 – NOVEMBER 13, 2008   www.flcourier.com

SPECIAL ELECTION ISSUE

AND STILL WE RISE!

Barack Hussein Obama becomes America's 44th president with a broad-based voter coalition and near-unanimous Black support

OLIVIER DOULIERY/ABACA PRESS/MCT

President-elect Barack Obama, daughters Sasha 7, Malia, 10, and wife Michelle will become America's first African-American first family.

13

This statewide African American newspaper's headline echoed a Maya Angelou poem, "And Still I Rise."

COMPILED FROM STAFF AND WIRE REPORTS

Barack Obama won the presidency Tuesday, the first African-American to claim the highest office in the land, an improbable candidate fulfilling a once-impossible dream by attracting an unprecedented voter coalition.

Obama won crucial swing states from the Rust Belt to the Mountain West. After TV media networks projected an Obama win at approximately 11 p.m. Tuesday night, Republican John McCain conceded shortly after polls closed on the West Coast as Black Americans rejoiced around the nation.

From the cafes of Beirut, Lebanon, to the villages of Kenya and on to the streets of Asian metropolises, much of the world looked on with vivid hope Wednesday at Obama's electoral triumph.

Some saw the rise of a Black American to the U.S. presidency as a transformative event that may repair the battered reputation of the United States, lift the aspirations of non-Whites worldwide, and renew chances for diplomacy rather than war.

Record turnout

Americans voted in record numbers, standing in lines that snaked around blocks and in some places in pouring rain. Voters who lined up on Tuesday and the millions who cast early ballots propelled what one expert said was the highest turnout in a century.

Michael McDonald of George Mason University estimates a 64.1 percent turnout rate, the highest turnout rate since 1908. Stephen Ansolabehere, a political science professor at Harvard and MIT, determined via exit polling data that Whites made up 74 percent of the 2008 electorate. That's down considerably from 81 percent in 2000 because of increase in Black and Hispanic voting, he said.

New voters, Blacks, youth

About seven in 10 first-time voters voted for Obama. Two-thirds of new voters were under age 30, one in five were Black and nearly as many were Hispanic.

The swell in youthful voters was largely due to the excitement about a new role model, the possibility of making history, and Obama's stand on the issues, said Melanie Campbell, president and CEO of the National Coalition for Black Civic Participation.

"The issues of the day such as Katrina and what happened on the Gulf Coast had an impact in 2006. We were upset and angry, but we also understood politically that we had to weigh in on the process," Campbell said.

The Joint Center for Political and Economic Studies determined last year that the top issues

Please see PRESIDENT, Page A2

Black Floridians greet news with tears, cheers

Change quickly seems real as voters watch election results unfold

COMPILED FROM STAFF REPORTS

Like so many Americans, Ila Woodward and her family woke up early Tuesday morning with one thought on their mind – to head to a voting precinct in search of "change they could believe in."

Woodward, her sister Lee Glasco and their 68-year-old mother were the first at their Tampa voting precinct.

"It was important for us to be 1, 2, and 3" in line to vote, Woodward told the Florida Courier Tuesday. "Once I got the voting done, I went in a quiet corner and cried."

'New global citizen'

The two sisters found a fitting place to witness change and watch Sen. Barack Obama make history. They were among a large, jubilant crowd gathered at Ybor City's Good Luck Café.

As the returns were flashed on CNN and the predominantly Black crowd cheered and danced, the sisters reflected on what the change would mean for them and the world, calling Obama "the new global citizen."

DELROY COLE/FLORIDA COURIER

South Florida residents track election returns at Hallandale's Gulfstream Park at a watch party sponsored by HOT 105 FM and the nationally syndicated "The Michael Baisden Show."

"I think it's going to be a major change in everyone's life," Glasco reflected. "He has given everybody hope."

No excuse now

Just a short drive away, first-time voter Jarod Walters celebrated with a diverse group near Busch Gardens who had gathered to support Obama. "I have never seen anything

like that before. It was like we won the Super Bowl. Everyone was happy and excited," he told the Florida Courier.

"Before Obama ran for the presidency, I used to feel the government was biased toward certain people. Now I feel there's no excuse for not realizing your dream of what you want to accomplish as an

Please see FLORIDIANS, Page A2

ALSO INSIDE

EDITORIAL | ANTHONY L. HALL: GOOD MORNING, MR. PRESIDENT-ELECT | A4

SPORTS | RICKIE WEEKS SR. HELPING FLORIDA YOUNGSTERS THRIVE AT BASEBALL | B5

0 94922 50897 3

14

A front-page story noted how Hispanic support factored into Obama's win of the nation's largest swing state. Hispanics flipped from 56 percent support for President George W. Bush in 2004 to 57 percent for Obama in 2008.

CONSTITUTIONAL AMENDMENTS – STORY, 1B

GAY MARRIAGE BAN LIKELY; COLLEGE MEASURE FAILS

The Miami Herald

35¢ MIAMI-DADE, 50¢ MONROE
106TH YEAR, NO. 52 ©2008

MiamiHerald.com

WEDNESDAY, NOV. 5, 2008
FINAL EDITION

D2

PRESIDENT OBAMA

PRESIDENTIAL RACE: FLORIDA PART OF NATIONAL TIDE FOR ILLINOIS SENATOR
BALANCE OF POWER: DEMOCRATS STRENGTHEN GRIP ON U.S. HOUSE, SENATE

NIKKI KAHN/THE WASHINGTON POST

THE WINNER: Sen. Barack Obama, accompanied by his wife, Michelle, and their two daughters, arrives at Grant Park in downtown Chicago for his victory rally.

3 INCUMBENTS PREVAIL

PEDRO PORTAL/EL NUEVO HERALD

Miami's trio of Cuban-American congressional Republicans withstood the toughest, best-financed challenges of their political careers on Tuesday, despite a wave of Democrats turning out.
● With 100 percent of precincts reporting, Rep. Mario Diaz-Balart had narrowly defeated Democratic Party activist Joe Garcia, 127,058 to 113,495.
● Rep. Lincoln Diaz-Balart (above) cruised to an easy victory over former Hialeah Mayor Raul Martinez, 132,861 to 97,184.
● Rep. Ileana Ros-Lehtinen vanquished political newcomer Annette Taddeo, 137,809 to 100,923.
STORY, 1B

1st black president makes U.S. history

BY BETH REINHARD
breinhard@MiamiHerald.com

Barack Obama will stride into the White House and the history books as the nation's first black president, riding a surge in Democratic voter registration, a tide of discontent with the Republican Party and a hard-fought triumph in Florida.

"If there is anyone out there who still doubts that America is a place where all things are possible, who still wonders if the dream of our founders is alive in our time, who still questions the power of our democracy, tonight is your answer," declared the 47-year-old Illinois senator to an emotional crowd estimated at 150,000 in Grant Park in Chicago. "Tonight, because of what we did on this day, in this election, at this defining moment, change has come to America."

Republican John McCain offered a gracious concession speech that recognized Obama's barrier-breaking achievement for African-Americans. He urged the country to unite.

*TURN TO OBAMA, 4A

How a shift in state boosted Democrat

BY MARC CAPUTO AND ROB BARRY
mcaputo@MiamiHerald.com

Buoyed by massive black support and the crucial votes of Hispanics, Democrat Barack Obama captured Florida by winning on the issues and striking deep into Republican strongholds.

Obama's Florida win over John McCain was a stinging loss for Republicans who control the Legislature and governor's mansion and, until just two months ago, were openly questioning whether the Democrat would campaign full force in the nation's biggest swing state.

But hard financial times, McCain's gaffe in Jacksonville where he said the "fundamentals of the economy are strong" and Obama's juggernaut of a campaign inalterably changed the race.

Obama beat McCain by a 51-48 percent margin, and captured a lopsided share of Florida votes from young people and first-time voters, winning comfortably among independents, and by besting McCain among Hispanic voters by double digits, according to Edison Media

*TURN TO SHIFT, 6A

The new political picture

Partial, unofficial election results by the numbers:

PRESIDENT

BARACK OBAMA	51%
Electoral votes	338
JOHN McCAIN	47%
Electoral votes	156

U.S. SENATE

DEMOCRATS	56
REPUBLICANS	40

U.S. HOUSE (projected)

DEMOCRATS	260
REPUBLICANS	175

GOVERNORS

DEMOCRATS	29
REPUBLICANS	21

A milestone

For voters who lived through the civil rights movement, this historic race was about much more than the presidency. **10A.**

Cuba not only factor

For many Cuban-American voters in Miami-Dade, U.S. policy toward Cuba wasn't only factor. **10A.**

01105

For Customer Service call 1-800-843-4372

St. Petersburg Times

Florida's Best Newspaper

tampabay.com

[WEDNESDAY, NOV. 5, 2008]

TIDE OF HOPE

BARACK OBAMA ELECTED 44TH PRESIDENT

Florida voters joined Ohio, Pennsylvania and Virginia in catapulting Barack Obama to a historic victory. It is only the second time a Democrat has carried Florida in 32 years.

Getty Images

BY ADAM C. SMITH | *Times Political Editor*

THERE IS A TIDE IN THE AFFAIRS OF MEN which, taken at the flood, leads to fortune. That was Shakespeare, and on Tuesday America embraced the sentiment. It was an absolute flood. An African-American man named Barack Obama is now president-elect of the United States of America. In his youth and eloquence he upended the politics in this country and suggested there is a new way, a new day. Whether you celebrate this outcome or lament it, the American ideal is true: Anything is possible. We are today a very different country than yesterday. This is change.

15

Perhaps the most literary of headlines, an allusion to Shakespeare's "There is a tide in the affairs of men . . ." picks up in the story.

Election '08 at a glance

Paper ballots pass the test, but glitches plague Hillsborough. Page 3A

Florida voters add gay marriage ban to state Constitution. Page 1B

Elizabeth Dole loses as Democrats gain at least 5 seats in Senate. Page 4A

Complete coverage 2A-11A, 1B-5B and on tampabay.com

7 89067 19941 3

16

To capture the event's magnitude, editors used a panoramic view of Obama's victory speech in Chicago's Grant Park. Both presidential candidates campaigned heavily in communities along Interstate 4, including Orlando and Tampa, and Obama's victories there helped deliver the state.

Orlando Sentinel

Wednesday, November 5, 2008   **75¢**

'THIS IS YOUR VICTORY'

12-PAGE SPECIAL SECTION   UPDATES ON AJC.COM

The Atlanta Journal-Constitution

ELECTION2008

••• WEDNESDAY, NOV. 5, 2008 75¢

BARACK OBAMA | 44th president of the United States

HISTORIC WIN

18

As in other areas of the country, people in the Atlanta area waited in line for hours to vote early in the weeks leading up to the election. More than half of Georgia voters cast their ballots before Election Day.

MORRY GASH / Associated Press

President-elect **Barack Obama** takes the stage at his Election Night party in Chicago's Grant Park. Hundreds of thousands gathered in the area to hear the Illinois Democrat's first address after his win.

RICH ADDICKS / raddicks@ajc.com

After news of Sen. Barack Obama's victory, **Kecia Cunningham** cries with joy in the arms of **Steve Vaughn** at the state Democrats' party Tuesday night at Hyatt Regency in Atlanta.

INSIDE COLUMNIST REFLECTS

'Extraordinary times'

"I'm struggling to find my footing on an altered terrain, a landscape where a black man can be elected president of the United States. It's an exciting place, a hopeful and progressive place, but it's unfamiliar. I didn't expect to find myself here so soon." **Cynthia Tucker, A18**

U.S. ELECTS 1ST BLACK PRESIDENT IN 'VICTORY OF FAITH OVER FEAR'

By CAMERON McWHIRTER / cmcwhirter@ajc.com

When the Rev. Martin Luther King Jr. delivered his "I have a dream" speech in 1963, calling for equal rights for black Americans, he was never so bold as to suggest that one day a black man could become the nation's chief executive.

Forty-five years later, Barack Obama became the first African-American president of the United States after the longest, most expensive and largest election in the country's history.

"I think this is arguably one of the most important events in our lifetime," said Molly Lister, 21, a Northwestern University student among the hundreds of thousands gathered in and around Chicago's Grant Park to hear Obama speak on Tuesday night.

When news organizations declared Obama the victor, the crowds exploded in jubilation.

"Change has come to America," Obama declared before a backdrop of U.S. flags.

"We have overcome," declared a homemade banner waved by one man.

While the Democrats celebrated, Republican John McCain and his supporters gathered at a private resort in the senator's hometown of Phoenix to listen as he delivered a gracious concession speech.

"The American people have spoken and they have spoken clearly," McCain said.

Praising Obama, he said America has moved beyond the dark days of its racist past, and said, "there is no better evidence of this than the election of an African-American to the presidency of the United States."

McCain also offered condolences to Obama on the death of his grandmother, Madelyn Payne Dunham, who died

➤ Please see PRESIDENT, Page 10

Vol. 60, No. 310
Copyright ©2008
The Atlanta
Journal-Constitution

The AJC
uses recycled
newsprint

ELECTORAL VOTES	STATES CARRIED	STATES CARRIED	POPULAR VOTE		U.S. SENATE
338 Barack Obama - D	**Obama:** CA, CO, CT, DC, DE, FL, HI, IA, IL, MA, MD, ME, MI, MN, NH, NJ, NM, NV, NY, OH, OR, PA, RI, VA, VT, WA, WI	**McCain:** AL, AR, AZ, GA, ID, KS, KY, LA, MS, ND, NE, OK, SC, SD, TN, TX, UT, WV, WY	**51%** Barack Obama - D		**Georgia race closely watched** Incumbent Republican Sen. Saxby Chambliss (top left) was leading Democratic opponent Jim Martin, but the gap was narrowing late Tuesday night. **Page 6**
156 John McCain - R			**48%** John McCain - R		

7 22011 00002 1

OBAMA!

ELECTION 2008

Honolulu Star-Bulletin

WEDNESDAY NOVEMBER 5, 2008 • 50¢ ★

'EXTRAORDINARY'
8-PAGE COMMEMORATIVE SPECIAL | SEE SECTION E

RAIL

Rail transit rolls to victory

Oahu residents support the 20-mile steel-rail transit system from Kapolei to Ala Moana by a comfortable margin, despite a spirited campaign by opponents. >> **A3**

YES	146,764
NO	132,268

MAYOR

FL MORRIS / FMORRIS@STARBULLETIN.COM

Mayor Mufi Hannemann, with wife Gail, addressed supporters during his victory rally last night.

Hannemann wins re-election

Mayor Mufi Hannemann maintains a strong lead throughout the night against City Councilwoman Ann Kobayashi, who ran a last-minute campaign that highlighted her opposition to his rail-transit system plan. >> **A3**

HANNEMANN	162,740
KOBAYASHI	118,102

CONSTITUTIONAL CONVENTION

State voters defeat Con Con

Hawaii's voters soundly reject the convening of a state Constitutional Convention. They also oppose a proposal to lower the qualifying age for governor and lieutenant governor. >> **A5**

NO	269,567
YES	146,021
BLANK	19,880

LEGISLATURE

Galuteria beats Sen. Trimble

Waikiki Republican Sen. Gordon Trimble goes down in defeat at the hands of Brickwood Galuteria, former Hawaii Democratic Party chairman, with the Legislature still firmly in Democratic Party hands. >> **A4**

■ DEMOCRAT ■ REPUBLICAN

HOUSE SEATS		
45		6

SENATE SEATS		
23		2

MORE COVERAGE

U.S. CONGRESS: Democrats increase their ranks in Congress, picking up seats from the Canadian to the Mexican borders and ushering in a new era of Democratic power in Washington the party has not seen since the 1960s. >> **E7**
NEIGHBOR ISLANDS: Lawyer Billy Kenoi, a former aide to Mayor Harry Kim, defeats Kona Councilman Angel Pilago in the mayor's race, while Bernard Carvalho Jr. beats former Mayor JoAnn Yukimura on Kauai. >> **A2**
BOARD OF EDUCATION: Former law school dean Carol Mon Lee ousts 20-year incumbent Denise Matsumoto, while another newcomer, Janis Akuna, clinches an Oahu at-large seat. >> **A4**
HOW THE VOTING WENT: Heavy turnout at some precincts delays the first results, but precincts report few technical problems. Nearly 170,000 people voted early or via mail. >> **A5**

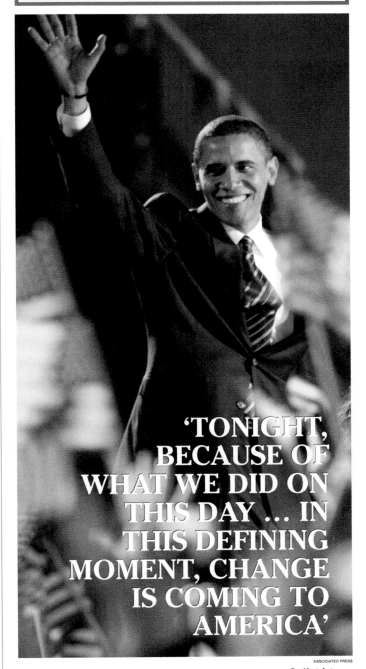

'TONIGHT, BECAUSE OF WHAT WE DID ON THIS DAY … IN THIS DEFINING MOMENT, CHANGE IS COMING TO AMERICA'

ASSOCIATED PRESS

President-elect Barack Obama waved to the huge crowd of supporters after giving his acceptance speech at Grant Park in Chicago last night.

HOW AMERICA VOTED

ELECTORAL VOTES
Needed to win: 270 of 538

Barack Obama	349
John McCain	147

 ELECTION RESULTS
PAGE E7

HOW HAWAII VOTED

Obama	McCain
311,669 **72%**	115,452 **27%**

HOW THE NATION VOTED*

Obama	McCain
56,954,765 **51.6%**	51,772,606 **47%**

(* 83% of votes cast)

19

Barack Obama was born in Honolulu, Hawaii, in 1961 and was raised by his mother and her parents. His maternal grandmother, Madelyn Dunham, died just before Election Day. Obama easily won the state.

THE 75 ARBITER

The Independent Student Voice of Boise State Since 1933

Thursday, November 06, 2008   Issue 25, Volume 21. First Issue Free

Obama, victorious

20

The college paper's illustrator started two versions of this painting but, based on early election night returns, focused on the one showing Obama winning.

ILLUSTRATION BY TONY MONTANO/THE ARBITER

Obama's improbable march into history is major, perhaps defining, turn on race

BY CHRISTI PARSONS
Chicago Tribune

Rosa Parks sat down. Martin Luther King Jr. marched. Barack Obama ran.

And Tuesday night, Obama's marathon reached an unprecedented place in American history.

The president-elect is an African-American, one whose face and words have come to define not just an election but a time in history.

A nation dedicated to the proposition that all men are created equal has elevated that principle to its highest office.

"This is a central moment in American history," Michael Dawson, one of the nation's leading authors and scholars on race and politics said. "Obama is an important signal to the world about the ability to overcome such a wretched history of conflict and hatred, and to build a more democratic society through the sweat and tears of its people."

On its face, the achievement is plain. An African-American will soon be sworn in as president of a country built partly with the forced labor of black slaves. Michelle Obama, who unlike her husband is a descendant of American slaves, will become first lady.

The moment takes on an even richer meaning when considered in the context of modern culture and politics – especially if that is defined in terms of the Illinois senator's own life span.

His parents' generation saw institutionalized racism begin to crumble, as Jim Crow laws were felled one by one. In 1954 the Supreme Court decided that segregated schools violated the 14th Amendment to the Constitution, guaranteeing all citizens equal protection of the law.

Shortly after that the court decided that segregation on public buses was illegal, a development stirred by Rosa Parks' refusal to give up her seat in the whites-only section and King's ensuing bus boycott.

Still, when Obama was a child in Hawaii, the marriage of his parents - a white woman and a black man - was illegal in 16 other states. In some parts of the United States, encouraging blacks to vote could get a person killed. The Ku Klux Klan was in full rage.

Today it's tempting to see Obama's historic election as a closing chapter of the country's tormented racial story. It's hard to witness the tears of joy on the white, black and brown faces of his supporters and not sense the possibility of a new, more colorblind nation.

History warns against it.

"While it's a huge symbolic transformation of American politics, it doesn't mean that racial conflict and disadvantage [are] going to disappear," Dawson said.

Historians aren't the only ones mindful of that. At a rally Tuesday in Philadelphia, rapper Jay-Z uttered a line that has been picking up currency among black voters and politicians this year.

"Rosa Parks sat so Martin Luther King could walk," Jay-Z told the crowd. "Martin Luther King walked so Obama could run."

An anonymous black man on the "L" in Chicago put his own spin on it when he announced to a car full of strangers: "Rosa Parks sat down. Martin Luther King marched. Barack Obama ran. And my grandchildren will fly."

See Arbiter News Editor Colby Stream behind the scene at the polls at ArbiterOnline.com. He starts at 6 a.m. Tuesday, Nov. 4 and ends just after 2 a.m. Nov. 5.

Have trouble registering? Arbiter producer Marcus Heleker interviews a poll worker on student registration. Visit arbiteronline.com to see how poll workers accommodated students.

Visit arbiteronline.com to see video slideshows of student reactions to Barack Obama winning the presidency.

Election-themed crime?

Obama bumper stickers target for vandals

BY COLBY STREAM
News/BizTech Editor

One of the bumper stickers on Mat Vook's car reads: "After we rebuild Iraq, can we please rebuild New Orleans."

But that isn't the one someone defaced.

Approximately two weeks ago, Vook, who lives in the University Square, noticed that someone ripped his Barack Obama bumper sticker in half. He also noticed other cars were missing their Obama stickers.

A few weeks later, someone

> "I thought we were a better people than that. And unfortunately people come out of the woodwork at times like this."
>
> *-Hilary Ward*
> *College Democrats President*

wrote the 'N' word on another car's Obama sticker in the apartment park-

See Crime · page 3

Steve Mercado
shares his political journey

BY TABITHA KEILY
News/BizTech Coordinator

While on the surface he seems a regular college student in jeans and a T-shirt, the Barack Obama pins on his chest tell a different story.

Not only does Steve Mercado work as the Vice President for the Idaho chapter of the Young Democrats of America, he also went to the Democratic National Convention earlier this year as a delegate for Idaho.

"It was just incredible to be a part of history, be in the middle of all that," he said.

Mercado was selected to sit on stage in the center of the front row during Obama's acceptance speech on the last day of the convention.

"I got to take pictures with Michelle

Obama, Biden as well. There was a lot of cool people I got to meet," he said. "I was seats away from President Carter, just incredible people all around me."

Steve Mercado

Mercado also met Harry Reed and took pictures with Howard Dean and Chevy Chase. Back here in Boise a democratic watch party cheered when Mercado appeared on screen briefly.

The trip cost around $3,000, which came from fundraising, college loans and from close friends and family. He brought back shirts, buttons, signs and various other memorabilia that

See Mercado · page 2

THE CHICAGO JEWISH NEWS

November 7 - 13, 2008/9 Cheshvan 5769 ■ www.chicagojewishnews.com ■ One Dollar

THE JEWS AND

כן אנו יכולים

Kein Anu Yecholim - Yes We Can!

PRESIDENT OBAMA

This paper spoke to its audience by translating Obama's "Yes we can" slogan into Hebrew.

22

Planning for an Obama victory, the newspaper prepared this front page a week in advance. The Sun-Times produced 700,000 copies of this edition, more than twice its typical run.

CHICAGO SUN-TIMES

50¢ CITY & SUBURBS • $1 ELSEWHERE | WEDNESDAY, NOVEMBER 5, 2008 | suntimes.com

MR.
PRESIDENT

75¢ CITY & SUBURBS, $1.00 ELSEWHERE—162ND YEAR NO. 310 © CHICAGO TRIBUNE

C CN CS N NNW NRW NS NW S SSW W

Chicago Tribune

WEDNESDAY, NOVEMBER 5, 2008

Obama
Our next president

In capturing the White House, Barack Obama redrew the electoral map, winning a larger share of the popular vote than any Democrat since Lyndon Johnson in 1964. PHIL VELASQUEZ/TRIBUNE

Before a huge Grant Park crowd, President-elect Obama declares: 'Change has come to America.'

Barack Obama, son of an African man and a white woman from Kansas, a figure virtually unknown outside his home state of Illinois just five years ago, emphatically captured the presidency Tuesday night.

"America, we have come so far," Obama told cheering thousands in Grant Park. "We have seen so much. But there is so much more to do."

His implausible journey to become the nation's first African-American president began on a cold February day almost two years ago, as he entered the race for the White House. Obama had spent little time on the national stage and was the furthest thing from a traditional candidate. Among other things, he was an Afri-

can-American in a country still grappling with the question of race.

With his victory, America's tortured relationship with race has entered a new phase. The Obama presidency may be a sign that a country that all too recently tolerated segregation has moved irrevocably forward, or it may mean only that the nation is so hungry for change that it set racial struggles aside.

The challenges facing Obama are many, including wars in Iraq and Afghanistan, and a battered economy. He will confront them soon enough.

But Tuesday night was a time to marvel at a once-inconceivable moment in American history.

COMPLETE ELECTION COVERAGE INSIDE

23

The Tribune's endorsement of then–Illinois senator Barack Obama was its first ever of the Democratic Party's nominee for president.

THE STATE Journal Register

** 75¢

SPRINGFIELD, ILLINOIS

STAY CONNECTED WITH CONTINUOUS NEWS AT WWW.SJ-R.COM | THE OLDEST NEWSPAPER IN ILLINOIS ™

WEDNESDAY
NOVEMBER 5, 2008

U.S. SENATE	18TH DISTRICT	ELECTION 2008	CIRCUIT CLERK	CORONER
DICK DURBIN Defeats Steve Sauerberg. **67** percent (93% of precincts) **PAGE 17**	**AARON SCHOCK** Over Colleen Callahan. **59** percent (91% of precincts) **PAGE 17**	**NO TO CON-CON** Voters reject calling a state constitutional convention. **PAGE 17** **NO TO BOARD CUT** Voters reject cutting the Sangamon County Board. **PAGE 18**	**TONY LIBRI** Wins over Cecilia Tumulty. **53.5** percent (All precincts reporting) **PAGE 18**	**SUSAN BOONE** Defeats Aby Phoenix. **59** percent (All precincts reporting) **PAGE 18**

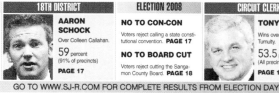

GO TO WWW.SJ-R.COM FOR COMPLETE RESULTS FROM ELECTION DAY

IT'S OBAMA

'CHANGE HAS COME TO AMERICA'

President-elect Barack Obama, his wife, Michelle, and daughters, Malia, 7, and Sasha, 10, wave to well-wishers in Chicago's Grant Park on Tuesday night.

Jae C. Hong/The Associated Press

24

The Springfield paper pointed out that Obama's candidacy for president began there on February 10, 2007, at the Old State Capitol, where he noted that President Abraham Lincoln "once called on a house divided to stand together."

Power, prestige of Illinois enhanced by senator's victory

History, pride and power.

For Illinois, all were enhanced Tuesday by the election of Barack Obama, the state's junior senator, as president of the United States.

"It's going to bring an enormous amount of prestige and power to this state," said state Treasurer Alexi Giannoulias.

"It'll probably get us the Olympics," Giannoulias said of Chicago's bid to host the Games in 2016. "And I think Illinois will be the Western White House."

Obama himself invoked history, turning several times in his acceptance speech to the words of one-time Springfield resident Abraham Lincoln and using Lincoln's words to reach out to those who did not back him for president.

"As Lincoln said to a nation far more divided than ours, 'We are not enemies, but friends,'" Obama said.

Obama also noted that Lincoln was the first person to "carry the Republican banner to the White House," and even a modern-day

BERNARD SCHOENBURG

Republican saw a bright side Tuesday in the victory of Obama, a Democrat.

Kent Gray of the Springfield suburb of Leland Grove, who was in Phoenix on Tuesday as an advance person for Republican vice presidential candidate Sarah Palin, said that, as president, Obama will fill thousands of federal jobs — many of them with long-time Illinois supporters or campaign workers.

"That'll create a vacuum" for Republicans to fill, said Gray.

Giannoulias said he considers that argument "silly," on the grounds that Illinois now is a strongly Democratic state.

State Comptroller Dan Hynes, who became an Obama supporter after losing the Democratic primary for U.S. Senate to Obama in 2004, also said the win "means a lot for Illinois, just as a source of pride, but also, hopefully as a source of Illinois being able to get what it needs out of the federal

See **SCHOENBURG** on page 10

Sen. John McCain concedes defeat in an appearance before supporters Tuesday night in Phoenix.

Chris Carlson/The Associated Press

Thousands celebrate

Barack Obama's supporters began gathering in Chicago's Grant Park hours before his victory.

PAGE 5

In search of stability

Bad news continues, but the financial world finds hope in the coming of a new administration.

PAGE 8

Around the country

■ Democrats gain at least five Senate seats.

■ Democrats expand their House majority.

■ Voters have a say on a number of issues.

■ Many voters wait for hours.

PAGE 4

Victory in campaign launched on steps of Old State Capitol

By DAVID ESPO
THE ASSOCIATED PRESS

WASHINGTON — A campaign that began on the steps of the Old State Capitol in Springfield ended Tuesday night with Barack Obama's election as the nation's first black president, overcoming racial barriers as old as America itself.

"Change has come to America," Obama told a cheering supporters in Chicago's Grant Park.

The son of a black father from Kenya and a white mother from Kansas, the Democratic senator from Illinois sealed his historic triumph by defeating Republican Sen. John McCain in a string of wins in hard-fought battleground states — Ohio, Florida, Virginia, Iowa and more.

On a night for Democrats to savor, they not only elected Obama the nation's 44th president but padded their majorities in the House and Senate, and come January will control both the White House and Congress for the first time since 1994.

Obama's election capped a meteoric rise — from state senator to

On the Web

▶ Photo gallery of Obama's historic victory.

▶ Video of political writer Bernard Schoenburg's analysis of Tuesday's races.

www.sj-r.com

president-elect in four years.

Spontaneous celebrations erupted from Atlanta to New York and Philadelphia as word of Obama's victory spread. A big crowd filled Pennsylvania Avenue in front of the White House.

In his first speech as victor, to more than 100,000 supporters in Chicago's Grant Park, Obama catalogued the challenges ahead. "The greatest of a lifetime," he said, "two wars, a planet in peril, the worst financial crisis in a century."

He added, "There are many who won't agree with every decision or policy I make as president, and we know that government can't solve

See **OBAMA** on page 10

INDEX							
ADVICE	13	ENTERTAINMENT	15	OPINION	6		
BUSINESS	8	FOOD	11	POLICE BEAT	20		
CITY/STATE	17	FOR THE RECORD	20	PUZZLES	24		
CLASSIFIED	22	HOROSCOPE	24	SPORTS	27		
COMICS	14	OBITUARIES	21	TV LISTINGS	15		

WEB SITE

sj-r.com
Stay connected with continuous news.

WEATHER

77 HIGH

Sunny today; a thunderstorm tonight. Winds 15-25 mph.
More on PAGE 32

55 LOW

Delivery questions?
Call 788-1440

© 2008, The State Journal-Register, GateHouse Media, Inc. All rights reserved. Our 177th year. No. 361

THE NEWSPAPER IOWA DEPENDS UPON | WEDNESDAY, NOVEMBER 5, 2008 | 75¢ | METRO EDITION

The Des Moines Register

OBAMA

AMERICA MAKES HISTORIC CHOICE FOR CHANGE

EMMANUEL DUNAND/GETTY IMAGES

25

The Register noted that Iowa delivered Obama's first victory in his bid for the Democratic nomination: "After the hands of Iowa Democrats shot up at January's caucuses, the nation's hands followed."

OBAMA'S ELECTORAL VOTES

367
POPULAR VOTE: 52,977,936

McCAIN'S ELECTORAL VOTES

167
POPULAR VOTE: 48,913,869

Barack Obama first tapped into what Iowans believed was possible.

And it turned out Tuesday that America believes it, too.

Obama will become the 44th president of the United States — and the country's first black president — after his decisive Electoral College victory Tuesday over John McCain.

"I hear your voices," Obama told a nationwide television audience and more than 100,000 supporters gathered at Grant Park in Chicago.

Iowa, which voted for Republican George W. Bush in 2004, was one of the key states that swung Obama's way,

along with Ohio, Florida and Virginia.

"It began in the backyards of Des Moines," Obama, 47, recalled Tuesday.

After the hands of Iowa Democrats shot up at January's caucuses, the nation's hands followed. The voices of change and hope grew loud enough to drown out the politics of old, even as new economic challenges appeared.

And Obama's first message to Americans as president-elect invoked the words of Lincoln and echoed John F. Kennedy.

"Let us summon a new spirit of patriotism, of service and responsibility where each of us resolves to pitch in and work harder," Obama said Tuesday night.

Iowa's Role

Election of a lifetime

Some Iowa residents thought they wouldn't live to see a black man elected president. "I never thought I'd see anything like this. Never." **Marc Hansen's column, Page 6A**

What mattered to Iowans

Across the state, it was a day of tears, a day to take action as Iowans went to the polls. **Article, Page 18A**

HOW IOWA VOTED

OBAMA	McCAIN
54%	45%

18 PAGES OF ELECTION COVERAGE: Iowa's congressional incumbents barely break a sweat as voters re-elect Sen. Tom Harkin and all five congressmen by healthy margins. **Pages 10A-12A.**

MORE ONLINE: Go to DesMoinesRegister.com to participate in a live chat with former Iowa Gov. Tom Vilsack today at 10 a.m. to hear his thoughts on the election. More online features, **Page 2A**

26

Obama's victory in Indiana, where he won 67 percent of first-time voters, was the first for a Democratic presidential candidate since Lyndon Johnson.

CONGRESS
Mike Pence to serve another term in U.S. House, page 3

'Change
s come to America'

27

E
n Daniels wins
her term as governor,
5

PRESIDENTIAL
Obama takes more than
300 electoral votes,
page 6

CAMPUS
Students react to
presidential voting results,
pages 7 and 8

THE TOPEKA CAPITAL-JOURNAL

WEDNESDAY | **NOVEMBER 5, 2008**

www.cjonline.com | **75 CENTS**

U.S. SENATE	**U.S. HOUSE**	**DISTRICT ATTORNEY**	**COUNTY COMMISSION**
Sen. Pat Roberts holds off challenge from Jim Slattery	State Treasurer Lynn Jenkins unseats Rep. Nancy Boyda	Chad Taylor defeats veteran prosecutor Eric Rucker	Incumbents Vic Miller and Ted Ensley win re-election

Complete elections coverage, Pages 2A, 6A, 7A, 8A and 1B. For more stories, photos, videos and reader comments, go to cjonline.com.

FACE OF CHANGE

Sen. Barack Obama defeated Sen. John McCain to win the presidential election and will make history in January when he is sworn in as the first black president.

THE ASSOCIATED PRESS

28

Although Obama lost Kansas, it was one of several states and countries that could lay claim to the president-elect because of his roots there.

In defeating McCain, Obama will be nation's first black president

By David Espo
THE ASSOCIATED PRESS

WASHINGTON — Barack Obama swept to victory as the nation's first black president Tuesday night in an electoral college landslide that overcame racial barriers as old as America itself.

"Change has come," Obama told to a huge throng of jubilant supporters in Chicago.

The son of a black father from Kenya and a white mother from Kansas, the Democratic senator from Illinois sealed his historic triumph by defeating Republican Sen. John McCain in a string of wins in hard-fought battleground states — Ohio, Florida, Virginia, Iowa and more.

On a night for Democrats to savor, they not only elected Obama the nation's 44th president

but padded their majorities in the House and Senate, and come January they will control both the White House and Congress for the first time since 1994.

Obama's election capped a meteoric rise — from mere state senator to president-elect in four years.

In his first speech as victor, to thousands at

Grant Park in his home town of Chicago, Obama catalogued the challenges ahead.

"The greatest of a lifetime," he said, "two wars, a planet in peril, the worst financial crisis in a century."

He also said: "There are many who won't agree

Please see **OBAMA**, *Page 9A*

Taylor surges to D.A.'s office

By Steve Fry
THE CAPITAL-JOURNAL

Political newcomer Chad Taylor took an early lead Tuesday night and built on it, beating veteran prosecutor Eric Rucker to win the Shawnee County district attorney's race.

With all precincts reporting, Taylor got 47,240 votes to 32,466 for Rucker, a split of 59.2 percent to 40.7 percent.

At 10 p.m., Rucker, the Republican candidate, conceded the election to Taylor, a Democrat.

At the same time Rucker conced-

ed the race, Taylor was speaking to a screaming, clapping crowd at the Democratic watch party at the Ramada Hotel and Convention Center after Larry Gates, state Democratic chairman, introduced him as the new district attorney.

At that point, Taylor hadn't heard from Rucker, but Gates said he "was pretty comfortable introducing to you the next district attorney, Chad Taylor."

Much of what Taylor said was

Please see **TAYLOR**, *Page 7A*

ANTHONY S. BUSH/THE CAPITAL-JOURNAL

Chad Taylor won his bid for Shawnee County district attorney, defeating Eric Rucker.

Jenkins ousts incumbent Boyda

By Tim Carpenter
THE CAPITAL-JOURNAL

Kansas Treasurer Lynn Jenkins proved Tuesday night her primary victory was no fluke.

The Republican orchestrated a stunning November surprise by upsetting Rep. Nancy Boyda, D-Kan., who lost her House seat after a single term representing Topeka, Manhattan and west Lawrence in the 2nd Congressional District. Jenkins capped a campaign that blossomed after her August primary triumph over former Rep. Jim Ryun.

"We had some tense and lively

discussions during this campaign and I think we engaged Kansans with the issues of the day, and because of it, the 2nd District is better off," Jenkins told supporters before midnight in Topeka.

Republican Sen. Pat Roberts, of Dodge City, easily earned re-election. GOP Reps. Jerry Moran, of Hays, and Todd Tiahrt, of Goddard, attained victory. Democratic Rep. Dennis Moore, of Lenexa, secured a new term.

Boyda, targeted by the national

Please see **JENKINS**, *Page 6A*

7 93258 00006 8

Index

Advice/Crossword 6B	Deaths & Funerals 3B	Sports 1D
Classified 4C	Flavor 1C	Stocks 1B
Comics 7B	Movies 3C	TV 6B
Daily Record 2B	Opinion 4A	Today 1B

Weather

Today: Chance of showers with a strong southern wind; high 71.
Tonight: Expect strong storms; low 47.
Full report, 5A

Contact us

Questions about delivery?
Call (785) 295-1133.
www.cjonline.com

LEO

NOVEMBER 12, 2008
FREE

IN GOD WE TRUST

LIBERTY

2009

CHANGE

DESIGN BY BRITTANY BAKER, BEN SCHNEIDER & JON BLEDSOE

NEWS: Metro Council hearts Cordish (mostly) — **PAGE 9**   **DINING:** One down, one up for Seviche — **PAGE 26**

29

This free alternative newsweekly used a photo illustration to capture the concept of change.

30

The Times-Picayune

BREAKING NEWS AT NOLA.COM — WEDNESDAY, NOVEMBER 5, 2008 — METRO EDITION · 75¢

THE 44th PRESIDENT

	BARACK OBAMA	JOHN McCAIN
POPULAR	**52%**	**47%**
ELECTORAL	**349**	**159**

IN HISTORIC RUN, OBAMA WINS WHITE HOUSE

PABLO MARTINEZ MONSIVAIS / THE ASSOCIATED PRESS

By Michael D. Shear and Robert Barnes The Washington Post

WASHINGTON

Sen. Barack Obama of Illinois was elected the nation's 44th president Tuesday, riding a reformist message of change and an inspirational exhortation of hope to become the first African-American to ascend to the White House.

Obama, 47, the son of a Kenyan father and a white mother from Kansas, led a tide of Democratic victories across the nation in defeating Republican Sen. John McCain of Arizona, a 26-year veteran of Washington who could not overcome his connections to President Bush's increasingly unpopular administration.

Standing before a crowd of more than 125,000 that had waited for hours at Chicago's Grant Park, Obama acknowledged the accomplishment and the dreams of his supporters.

"If there is anyone out there who still doubts that America is a place where all things are possible, who still wonders if the dream of our founders is alive in our time, who still questions the power of our democracy, tonight is your answer," he said just before 11 p.m.

"The road ahead will be long. Our climb will be steep. We may not get there in one year or even one term, but America, I have never been more hopeful than I am tonight that we will get there. I promise you: We as a people will get there."

The historic Election Day brought millions of new and sometimes tearful voters, long lines at polling places nationwide, and celebrations on street corners and in front of the White House. It ushered in a new era of Democratic dominance in Congress, even

See **PRESIDENT,** *A-9*

President-elect Barack Obama acknowledges the cheers and tears of thousands as he takes the stage at his election night party in Grant Park, Chicago, on Tuesday.

U.S. SENATE

MARY LANDRIEU	963,905	52%
JOHN KENNEDY	855,723	46%

Landrieu takes a third term

By Ed Anderson and Bill Barrow Capital bureau

Once targeted by national Republicans as the U.S. Senate's most vulnerable Democratic incumbent, Sen. Mary Landrieu defeated GOP state Treasurer John Kennedy on Tuesday to claim a third term.

Landrieu, who won by narrow margins in 1996 and 2002, took a slightly more comfortable victory against the backdrop of her diminished Democratic base of pre-Katrina New Orleans.

Joined by her large family and former

See **LANDRIEU,** *A-15*

HOUSE, 1ST DISTRICT

STEVE SCALISE	178,355	66%
JIM HARLAN	91,589	34%

Scalise wins 1st District

By Mary Sparacello Kenner bureau

U.S. Rep. Steve Scalise turned back an aggressive $1.3 million challenge from Jim Harlan on Tuesday to win a full term representing the congressional 1st District.

"This has been a hard-fought campaign," Scalise, 43, told backers at Andrea's restaurant in Metairie. "The last few months have been a really challenging time for my family."

Scalise, a Republican from Old Jefferson, served 12 years as a state legislator, then

See **SCALISE,** *A-26*

HOUSE, 2ND DISTRICT

WILLIAM JEFFERSON	83,211	56%
HELENA MORENO	65,230	44%

Jefferson beats Moreno

By Frank Donze and Michelle Krupa Staff writers

With his trial on federal corruption charges looming and questions swirling about his effectiveness in Congress, U.S. Rep. William Jefferson cruised to an easy victory Tuesday in the Democratic Party runoff for the 2nd Congressional District.

The decisive win over Helena Moreno, a former TV news anchor and political newcomer, ensures Jefferson a spot in the Dec. 6 general election. With two-thirds of the district's voters registered as Democrats,

See **JEFFERSON,** *A-20*

OTHER RACES

COMPLETE ELECTION COVERAGE BEGINS ON A-9

STATE PAGE A-25
ERIC SKRMETTA
PUBLIC SERVICE COMMISSION

JEFFERSON PARISH PAGE A-24
ELLEN KOVACH
24TH JUDICIAL DISTRICT COURT, DIVISION K

NEW ORLEANS PAGE A-22
LEON CANNIZZARO
DISTRICT ATTORNEY

ST. TAMMANY PARISH PAGE A-30
REJECTED
ONE-QUARTER CENT SALES TAX

172ND YEAR
NO. 289

WEDNESDAY 11.05.08

F 75¢

THE BALTIMORE SUN

LIGHT FOR ALL

baltimoresun.com

Our 171st year, No. 310   Informing more than 1 million Maryland readers weekly in print and online

It's Obama

Democrat gains historic victory, will be the nation's first black president

Barack Obama
NATIONAL VOTE
51.5%
ELECTORAL VOTES
338

John McCain
NATIONAL VOTE
47.2%
ELECTORAL VOTES
141
79 percent reporting

CONGRESS
BLUE STREAK FOR HOUSE, SENATE: Democrats tapped into a sour economy, antipathy toward Bush as they chased larger majorities in both bodies. **Election PG 8**

1ST DISTRICT
KRATOVIL (right)
49%
HARRIS (left)
48%
93 percent reporting

TURNOUT
ENTHUSIASTIC AND EARLY IN MARYLAND: Voters participated in what experts say may be Maryland's biggest turnout for a presidential election since World War II. **Election PG 1**

SPECIAL SECTION
Twelve pages of results, coverage, analysis and photos from Maryland and accross the nation. **Election section inside**

ONLINE
Find analysis, developments and updated election results at baltimoresun.com

ELECTORAL LANDSLIDE President-elect Barack Obama greets the crowd in Chicago's Grant Park after his overwhelming victory over John McCain turned the page on eight years of Republican leadership. PHOTOS: ASSOCIATED PRESS

BY DAVID NITKIN | david.nitkin@baltsun.com

Barack Obama, the Illinois Democrat who built a campaign and a movement around the promise of change, won a resounding victory over Republican John McCain last night to become the first black president in U.S. history.

Choosing a steady 47-year-old lawyer and former community organizer to guide the nation, voters looked past Obama's relative lack of national experience to end eight years of Republican leadership amid a once-in-a-century economic crisis and protracted foreign wars.

Hundreds of thousands of supporters gathered in Grant Park in Chicago, which Obama represented in the Illinois Legislature just 46 months ago, as the Democrat was declared the winner about 11 p.m. Eastern time.

Obama said that his victory reaffirmed that America remains a place "where all things are possible."

"It's been a long time coming, but tonight, because of what we did on this date, in this election, at this defining moment, change has come to America," he said.

Celebrations erupted in New York, Washington, Baltimore, Atlanta and other cities.

The son of a mother from Kansas and a father from Kenya, Obama becomes the first U.S. senator to be elected president since John F. Kennedy in 1960. The 44th president will take office at a time of daunting challenges, amid an economic crisis that threatens to overwhelm his promises to spend on education, health care and energy. See **PRESIDENT,** election 5

Republican John McCain, who campaigned as a maverick, never shook the burden of representing the party of President Bush.

A new American majority takes shape

BY PAUL WEST | paul.west@baltsun.com

WASHINGTON
America turned a page yesterday.

Barack Obama broke through the racial barrier to the Oval Office, becoming the first African-American to gain the presidency. And his electoral landslide delivered a powerful message about a new generation of American leadership.

The young and minority voters who helped lift the 47-year-old Democrat to the White House are now the foundation of a new majority in U.S. politics. Their emergence likely brings to a close the era of conservative dominance that began with Ronald Reagan's election almost three decades ago.

analysis

Obama's campaign, perhaps the most brilliantly run in the modern era, reflected the multicultural diversity of 21st-century America. He sought to move beyond old racial divides, but his victory also means that a descendant of slaves will become first lady of the United States for the very first time.

"A new dawn of American leadership is at hand," the president-elect said last night. "To those who would tear this world down — we will defeat you. To those who seek peace and security — we support you. And to all those who have wondered if America's beacon still burns as bright — tonight we proved once more that the true strength of our nation comes not from the might of our arms or the scale of our wealth, but from the enduring See **ANALYSIS,** election 6

end of debate

Md. voters give OK to 15,000 slots

Strong majority backs constitutional change

BY LAURA SMITHERMAN
laura.smitherman@baltsun.com
AND GADI DECHTER
gadi.dechter@baltsun.com

Marylanders voted overwhelmingly yesterday to legalize slot-machine gambling in the state after a rancorous campaign, dealing Gov. Martin O'Malley a ballot-box success and settling a debate over which politicians had deadlocked for years.

The constitutional amendment to allow 15,000 slot machines at five locations around the state appeared headed for easy passage late last night.

FOR
59%

AGAINST
41%
85 percent reporting

O'Malley, a Democrat, championed slots as a way to plug the state's budget shortfalls, made worse by a declining economy, while opponents argued that expanding gambling would invite crime and addiction into the most vulnerable communities and burden taxpayers with increased social costs. The final say fell to voters after state lawmakers decided last year to punt the decision to a referendum.

Voter opinions varied from liberal, anti-slots enclaves in the Washington suburbs to See **SLOTS,** election 10

inside   lottery **news 4** • crime & courts **news 6** • business maryland **news 18** • obituaries **news 22**
opinion **news 24** • classified **sports 7** • movies **you 5** • crossbords **you 6, sports 12** • tonight on tv **you 6**

31

Obama's popularity helped Democrats secure seven of Maryland's eight House districts, and backers of a successful effort to approve slot-machine gambling used his image on Election-Day placards.

VOLUME 274
NUMBER 128

Suggested retail price
75 cents
$1.00 outside of
Greater Boston

The Boston Globe

WEDNESDAY, NOVEMBER 5, 2008

RESOLUTION
TODAY: *Early fog, cloudy, rain later.*
High 61-66. Low 49-54.
TOMORROW: *Cloudy, a sprinkle.*
High 57-62. Low 50-55.

HIGH TIDE: *3:58 a.m. 4:06 p.m.*
SUNRISE: *6:23 a.m.* SUNSET: *4:32 p.m.*
FULL REPORT: PAGE C8

Historic victory

ELECTORAL COLLEGE Obama 338 |142

270 NEEDED TO WIN

Obama elected nation's first African-American president in a romp

McCain falters on GOP terrain; Democrats increase clout in Congress

JASON REED/REUTERS

President-elect Barack Obama, his daughters Sasha and Malia, and wife Michelle waved to supporters last night in Chicago's Grant Park.

32

In its October

endorsement of

Obama, the Globe

said of the Harvard

Law School

graduate: "The

United States has to

dig itself out. Barack

Obama is the one to

lead the way."

**By Scott Helman
and Michael Kranish**
GLOBE STAFF

CHICAGO — Senator Barack Obama of Illinois was elected the 44th president of the United States and the nation's first black commander in chief yesterday, his triumph ushering in an era of profound political and social realignment in America.

Obama's decisive victory over Republican John McCain is a landmark in the country's 232-year history, especially for the millions of African-Americans around the country energized and inspired by his improbable candidacy. It gives Democrats control of Congress and the White House for the first time in 16 years and it led to impromptu celebrations around the country.

Making good on his promise to draw his own electoral map, Obama captured Virginia, which last voted for a Democrat in 1964, and he beat McCain in key battleground states, including Colorado, Florida, New Hampshire, Ohio, and Pennsylvania, while holding on to Democratic-leaning states. He won in part on the support of new voters, African-Americans, and Hispanics, and as of early today he had 338 electoral votes, far more than the 270 needed to win the presidency, while McCain had 142.

In a grand celebration on a balmy fall night in Chicago's Grant Park, 240,000 supporters gathered to toast the president-elect. When the networks called the race shortly after 10 p.m. local time, tears flowed, flashbulbs

ELECTION, Page A12

New era beginning for party in power

By Susan Milligan
GLOBE STAFF

WASHINGTON — Democrats increased their ranks in Congress last night, picking up seats from the Canadian to the Mexican borders and ushering in a new era of Democratic power in Washington the party has not seen since the 1960s.

In a heavy blow to the GOP, Democrats collected several high-profile Senate seats, ousting veteran Republican lawmaker John Sununu in New Hampshire and replacing him with former governor Jeanne Shaheen. New Mexico and Colorado sent two Democratic brothers to the Senate, with Mark Udall taking the Colorado seat and Tom Udall winning the race in New Mexico.

In Virginia, Mark Warner easily defeated James Gilmore, his GOP opponent, capping a stunning Democratic showing in the Old Dominion State, which also voted for Barack Obama — the first time since 1964 that a Democratic presi-

CONGRESS, Page A15

ELECTORAL COLLEGE ◻ Obama wins ◻ Obama leading ■ McCain wins ▪ McCain leading

[Electoral map of the United States]

WA 11, OR 7, MT 3, ND 3, MN 10, WI 10, MI 17, NY 31, NH 4, VT 3, ME, MA 12, RI 4, CT 7, NJ 15, DE 3, DC 3, MD 10, ID 4, WY 3, SD 3, IA 7, IL 21, IN 11, OH 20, PA 21, WV, VA 13, NV 5, UT 5, CO 9, NE 5, KS 6, MO 11, KY 8, TN 11, NC 15, SC 8, CA 55, AZ 10, NM 5, OK 7, AR 6, MS 6, AL 9, GA 15, TX 34, LA 9, FL 27, HI 4, AK 3

Election 2008

JIM WATSON/AFP/GETTY IMAGES

John McCain said he gave his all, while aides said his trouble began when he declared the teetering economy sound. **A14.**

MARK WILSON/GLOBE STAFF

Lines were long at polling places across the nation, but Obama's prodigious field organization helped keep problems to a minimum. **A16.**

**Massachusetts voters reject-
ed a repeal** of the state income tax, said yes to decriminalizing possession of small amounts of marijuana, and approved a ban on greyhound racing. **B1.**

Senator John F. Kerry rolled to a fifth term over Republican Jeffrey K. Beatty amid speculation that Kerry would join the new administration. **B9.**

SAUL LOEB/AFP/GETTY IMAGES

Emotions ran high in Chicago as tens of thousands poured into Grant Park from near and far for Obama's acceptance speech. **A13.**

Sonia Chang-Díaz captured the seat long held by state Senator Dianne Wilkerson, who left the race after being arrested on bribery charges. **B9.**

Coverage, A12-17, B1, B6-10.

Have a news tip? E-mail newstip@globe.com or call 617-929-TIPS (8477). Other contact information, **B2.**

NEWS ANALYSIS

Shift in tone will bring a watershed for nation

By Peter Canellos
GLOBE STAFF

CHICAGO — The people who crowded Grant Park last night, straining for a glimpse of President-elect Barack Obama, were aroused by a lot of passionate issues — war, jobs, race — and yet they insisted that no single goal, nothing that could be written out and measured, defined their expectations for the next administration.

"It's everything," said a tearful Teri McClain of Seattle.

"It's having a president with a world view that most Americans can believe in," declared Chris Godfrey of Des Moines, Iowa.

And yet Obama's clear-cut victory, bolstered by strong majorities of his own party in both houses of Congress, can be read as a mandate for some very specific policy changes that could, by themselves, have momentous impact. Withdrawal from Iraq. Renewal of the six-decade quest for national health insurance. The launch of a major government-funded quest for renewable energy.

Beyond the policies, Obama's election will stand forever amid the great milestones of America's racial history, the end of a torturous progression from emancipation to the civil rights movement to the election of the first black

ANALYSIS, Page A13

Among blacks, joy and tears at journey's end

By Michael Levenson
GLOBE STAFF

Sixty-six-year-old Jake Coakley picked cotton as a boy in Beaufort, S.C., just as his father and grandfather did before him. So yesterday, as he stood amid a throng of people hugging, high-fiving, and even weeping outside a Roxbury polling place, he wanted to underscore the significance of the day.

"This," he said to a little boy, patting his head and staring deeply into his eyes, "is history."

At another polling station blocks away, Charles Robinson recalled the racial epithets shouted at him as a student at South Boston High School during the busing crisis of the 1970s.

In St. Petersburg, Fla., Ron Dock spoke of the day he learned that the Rev. Martin Luther King Jr. had been shot. Dock was 18, he said, crouching in a rice paddy in Vietnam, preparing for a firefight. In Alexandria, Va., 83-year-old Flossie Parks recalled turning 21 and being forced to pay a $3 poll tax for the right to vote.

Millions of black voters across the country turned out to help elect Barack Obama the first African-American president yesterday, and as they did, they reflected not just on the course of a historic campaign, but on the history of a nation.

BLACK VOTE, Page A17

For breaking news, updated Globe stories, and more, visit:

boston.com

Inside

Features
Business B11
Deaths B17-19
Editorials A18
Lottery B2
Weather C8
© Globe Newspaper Co.

Classified
Cars, Homes, Stuff, Notices & more J
g
TV/Radio, Comics, Crossword, Sudoku, KenKen, Movies, Horoscope

45340

0 94772 5 4

Detroit Free Press

■ IN-DEPTH COVERAGE ON FREEP.COM
■ INTERACTIVE U.S. VOTING MAP
■ LOCAL ELECTION RESULTS
■ VIDEOS AND LOTS OF PHOTOS

WWW.FREEP.COM WEDNESDAY NOV. 5, 2008 METRO FINAL ✦✦

Historic.
Decisive.
Once unthinkable.

Barack Obama captured the White House on Tuesday night as Americans, voting in record numbers, turned a page to the future and embraced a man who will become the nation's first African-American president.

Invoking a message of change and hope, he will lead a nation tested by wars in Iraq and Afghanistan and by an ailing economy symbolized in part by Michigan's struggling automakers and high unemployment.

He takes the reins of power as the 44th president after racking up victories in a string of battleground states and riding a Democratic wave that, to a great extent, reshapes the nation's political map. Republican John McCain, the former prisoner of war who called himself a maverick, conceded the election just after 11 p.m.

By Todd Spangler

A VOTE FOR CHANGE

RASHAUN RUCKER/Detroit Free Press
Brother and sister Laban and Edwina King of Detroit shed tears in celebration of Barack Obama's victory Tuesday at the Marriott Renaissance Hotel. "My father told me when I was a child, a black president was probably not realistic," Laban King said. "I can't believe it."

OLIVIER DOULIERY/McClatchy-Tribune
President-elect Barack Obama hugs his daughter Malia, 10, after giving his acceptance speech Tuesday night at Grant Park in Chicago.

OBAMA
THE NEXT PRESIDENT OF THE UNITED STATES

33

The paper reprinted its front page as a T-shirt and as a poster. Thousands lined up around the newspaper's building to get a copy of history.

16 PAGES OF COVERAGE IN 2 SECTIONS

THIS SECTION: The presidential race, U.S. House and Senate and other national races.

NEXT SECTION: Michigan ballot proposals and local races.

ELECTION 2008: WINNERS AND HEADLINES

KNOLLENBERG OUT: Peters takes the win. 8S
TAYLOR UPSET: Hathaway stuns justice. 7A
MEDICAL POT OK'D: Proposal 1 passes. 1A
PROP 2: Stem cell research passes. 1A
OAKLAND EXEC: Patterson cruises to win. 1A

ROCHELLE RILEY: Rewriting gravity's rules. 6S
STEPHEN HENDERSON: A stride, yes ... 2S
LEVIN ROMPS: Dem easily keeps his seat. 9S
OAKLAND PROSECUTOR: Cooper out ahead. 5A
DILLON SURVIVES: Recall try is defeated. 6A

Vol. 178, Number 185
© 2008
Detroit Free Press Inc.
Printed in the U.S.

50¢ Wayne, Oakland & Macomb counties | 75¢ Elsewhere

★★★★ ELECTION 2008 ★ 28 PAGES OF COVERAGE INSIDE

StarTribune
Wednesday • 50¢

StarTribune.com ↖
Get the latest results at **startribune.com**

NOVEMBER 5, 2008 • STARTRIBUNE.COM • MINNEAPOLIS • ST. PAUL • MINNESOTA'S TOP NEWS CHOICE

OBAMA

Supporters are euphoric as he promises era of change

Bitter Senate race between Coleman, Franken too close to call

"If there is anyone out there who still doubts that America is a place where all things are possible ... tonight is your answer," Barack Obama told a celebrating crowd in Chicago's Grant Park on Tuesday night.

JOE RAEDLE • Getty Images

34

At the site of the 2008 Republican National Convention, editors had to weigh the importance of the presidential election against a high-profile Senate race that was too close to call.

PRESIDENT

• The senator's "improbable quest" gained enough steam over two years to end in a historic victory.

By KEVIN DIAZ
kdiaz@startribune.com

Barack Obama, the multiracial son of a mother from Kansas and a father from Kenya, was elected Tuesday as the 44th president of the United States, writing a remarkable new chapter in American history with a campaign built on the theme of hope.

In a race that captivated the nation, and that climaxed in the gloom of an economic crisis, the closing of polls on the West Coast showed that what began as the Illinois senator's "improbable quest" nearly two years ago ended as a commanding electoral victory over Republican John McCain. The Arizona senator had struggled to defy the pollsters in the waning hours of the longest and most expensive presidential election ever.

"If there is anyone out there who still doubts that America is a place where all things are possible, who still wonders if the dreams of our founders are alive in our time, who still questions the power of our democracy, tonight is your answer," Obama told a huge, euphoric crowd in Chicago's Grant Park.

McCain conceded shortly after 10 p.m., saying, "Senator Obama has achieved a great thing for himself and for his country." As he spoke, spontaneous street celebrations erupted among Obama revelers

from Los Angeles to Times Square. In Grant Park, tens of thousands of Obama supporters wept, waved flags and chanted, "Yes we did!"

Obama became the first black man to win the presidency, reaching victory by stringing together a series of crucial wins in battleground states, including Florida, Pennsylvania and Ohio.

Obama also scored a decisive victory in Minnesota, the site of the Republican National Convention in September, a time when the state – which hasn't gone Republican in nine presidential elections – was still thought to be up for grabs.

Minnesotans, like voters across the nation, waited in long lines at many polls, with only sporadic reports of polling problems.

Black voters were particularly energized, among them Don Smith, 47, a north Minneapolis man who said he was witnessing one of the most important days in history.

His only regret, he said, was that his mother, who died in August, wasn't there with him.

"I just wish she was alive to see this," said Smith, who was in line to vote before 6 a.m.

Secretary of State Mark Ritchie said that he expected total voter turnout in Minnesota could surpass a record 3 million, more than 80 percent of the roughly 3.7 million eligi-

Obama continues on A8 ▶

ELECTORAL VOTES
As of 1:30 a.m.

Obama
349

McCain
145

MINNESOTA PRESIDENTIAL VOTE
86% of precincts

Obama
52%

McCain
47%

MINNESOTA SENATE VOTE
94% of precincts

Barkley
15%

Coleman
42%

Franken
42%

U.S. SENATE

With the race still in doubt late into the night, Al Franken said to DFL supporters: "What, you thought this was going to be easy?"

"There is more counting to be done," GOP Sen. Norm Coleman said. "Keep being hopeful. I'm feeling very good right now."

• With only a few thousand votes separating Coleman and Franken, a recount looms, perhaps delaying the result for days.

By PATRICIA LOPEZ
and KEVIN DUCHSCHERE
Star Tribune staff writers

One of the most bitter U.S. Senate races in Minnesota history continued to grind on early this morning, with Republican Sen. Norm Coleman and DFL challenger Al Franken locked in a race that remained too close to call.

With more than 90 percent of the returns in, Franken and Coleman were in a virtual tie well after midnight.

A winning margin of less than one half of 1 percent — about 15,000 votes — would trigger an automatic recount and could delay a result for days while ballots are

retabulated across the state.

Coleman was leading in the suburbs and southern Minnesota, but Franken was ahead in two reliable DFL strongholds — the central cities and Iron Range. A chunk of votes in Minneapolis and the Duluth area remained uncounted as this edition of the Star Tribune went to press.

Exit polls showed that Franken was helped by a wave of Democrats — including large numbers of first-time voters — who had already delivered the state's electoral votes to Democratic President-elect Barack Obama.

But Franken struggled through-

Senate continues on A16 ▶

AMENDMENT

Outdoor, arts sales tax is approved B1

SIXTH DISTRICT

Bachmann retains seat; Tinklenberg concedes A20

THIRD DISTRICT

Paulsen defeats Madia A20

TURNOUT

Heavy voting in Minnesota could break record A13

STAR TRIBUNE
Vol. XXVII • No. 215
Mpls., St. Paul Nov. 5, 2008

CONTACT US
Delivery 612.673.4343
News tips.............612.673.4414
Classified.............612.673.7000

FIND COMPLETE, UPDATED RESULTS WITH INTERACTIVE MAPS, VIDEOS OF VOTERS AND PHOTO GALLERIES AT STARTRIBUNE.COM

SunHerald

SOUTH MISSISSIPPI'S NEWSPAPER

50¢   VOL. 125, NO. 33   WEDNESDAY, NOVEMBER 5, 2008   www.sunherald.com

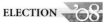 ELECTION '08

■ **Mississippi votes for John McCain, A-6**

■ **Gracious McCain calls for unity, C-1**

■ **Obama faces daunting list of challenges, C-1**

'CHANGE HAS COME TO AMERICA'

OBAMA WINS

U.S. ELECTS FIRST BLACK PRESIDENT

JAE C. HONG/THE ASSOCIATED PRESS

President-elect Barack Obama, his wife, Michelle, and their daughters, Malia, 7, and Sasha, 10, at the election night celebration in Chicago.

MORE INSIDE

■ Local Democrats rejoice in Obama win, **A-7**

■ Gene Taylor, Thad Cochran win re-election, **A-6**

■ Pierce wins seat on state Supreme Court, **A-6**

■ County-by-county election results, **A-8**

By STEVEN THOMMA
McCLATCHY NEWSPAPERS

WASHINGTON — Barack Obama was elected the 44th president of the United States on Tuesday, swept to victory by an anxious country eager to change course at home and abroad.

Obama, 47, becomes the first black in U.S. history to win the presidency and the first from the generation that came of age after the turbulence of the 1960s.

His win suggested a new political order in the making. He drew masses of young people to politics for the first time. His biracial heritage reflected the changing demographic face of America. His mastery of the Internet matched the rise of a new information age. And his push into formerly Republican states in the South, Midwest and West marked a new political landscape possibly emerging.

After an epic struggle, the first-term Democratic senator from Illinois defeated Republican John McCain, 72, a hero of the Vietnam War and a

Please see Obama, A-11

SUNHERALD TV

To see video from a South Mississippi voting precinct, go to **sunherald.com**

MORE ONLINE

For more photos of Election Day, go to **sunherald.com**

Wicker will keep his Senate seat

Musgrove refuses to concede

By MICHAEL NEWSOM
mnewsom@sunherald.com

Republican Roger Wicker proclaimed victory over former Democratic Gov. Ronnie Musgrove late Tuesday in the hotly contested battle for the seat formerly held by long-serving Republican Trent Lott.

But although Wicker made a victory speech, at press time, Musgrove's campaign refused to concede, saying it wasn't over until "all the votes are counted," as they had information there were likely tens of thousands of affidavit ballots in the state still to be counted.

At 91 percent reporting, Wicker received 56 percent of the vote to Musgrove's 44 percent, with a 119,079 vote margin. Surrounded by supporters and joined by Republican Gov. Haley Barbour at a downtown Jackson hotel, Wicker thanked his volunteers for their hard work.

"The people of Mississippi got out to vote in overwhelming

Please see Wicker, A-11

U.S. Sen. Roger Wicker, R-Miss., and his wife, Gayle, celebrate his victory over Democratic challenger, former Gov. Ronnie Musgrove, for the unfinished term of retired Republican Sen. Trent Lott, in Jackson.

ROGELIO V. SOLIS/
THE ASSOCIATED PRESS

FOR HOME DELIVERY, CALL 1-800-346-2472   ez√pay

RESULTS

U.S. Senate

Wicker   Musgrove
606,151   488,367
*97 percent of precincts reporting

Cochran   Fleming
675,796   417,350
*97 percent of precincts reporting

U.S. House

McCay   Taylor
67,600   198,518
*99 percent of precincts reporting

Supreme Court

Pierce   Diaz
207,615   148,865
*98 percent of precincts reporting

Jackson County

Jail bond

For   24,067
Against   20,683
*100 percent of precincts reporting

State races

U.S. House
District 1

T. Childers	166,740
G. Davis	136,237
W. Pang	3,338
J. Wages	1,668

*96 percent of precincts reporting

District 2

B. Thompson	172,269
R. Cook	83,505

*94 percent of precincts reporting

District 3

J. Gill	108,175
G. Harper	187,918

*97 percent of precincts reporting

SOUND OFF OF THE DAY

"I sure hope that whatever the outcome in this election that we can all stay sticking together, support one another and not become complete enemies. Let's be grown up and adult about this."
More Sound Offs, A-2

CORRECTION

■ Here are the weekly Wall Street numbers for the week ending Oct. 31: Dow Jones, 9,325.01, up 946.06; Nasdaq, 1,720.95, up 168.92; S&P 500, 968.75, up 91.98. Incorrect consolidated numbers were published on B-12 in Saturday's paper.

INDEX

Annie & Abby	C-8	Obituaries	A-4
Business	B-8	Opinion	C-6
The Buzz	C-12	Sports	B-1
Classified	D-1	Stocks	B-7
Comics	C-9	TV	C-8
Crosswords	D-5	World	C-1
Horoscope	C-8	Your Life	C-14

Warm
77° 60°
Weather, C-3

35

The Sun Herald *was one of many newspapers to use Obama's own words to capture what happened on Election Day: "Change has come to America."*

The paper sold out of its 262,000 November 5 press run, sold out of a 25,000-copy reprint the next day, and then printed a ten-page special section the following Sunday.

ELECTION SPECIAL
Terry defeats Esch in a close race for the 2nd District U.S. House seat.
Nebraskans approve affirmative action ban, but legal questions loom.

Omaha World-Herald

WEDNESDAY, NOVEMBER 5, 2008 / SUNRISE EDITION / AN INDEPENDENT NEWSPAPER OWNED BY EMPLOYEES

Face of change

U.S. voters turn out in historic numbers to elect the nation's first black president

It's a notion that speaks to this nation's very ideals, the one that says any child, no matter how humble his birth, could one day grow up to be president.

After Tuesday, that dream may have more currency than ever.

In what clearly will go down as a watershed election, energized American voters turned out in historic numbers Tuesday to elect Democrat Barack Obama the 44th president of the United States.

He's the son of an African immigrant father and a teen mother from Kansas. And he was born at a time black "freedom riders" were braving club-wielding mobs to promote civil rights in America's South. But in January, the 47-year-old Obama will take office as the nation's first black president.

His election also marks a stark shift in the political tides. The Democrat was even threatening to turn reliably red Nebraska "purple" in a sweeping national victory over John McCain, one that will be seen as a mandate for the change Obama has pledged.

"America, we have come so far. We have seen so much," Obama told tens of thousands of supporters in Chicago. "But there is so much more to do."

From the moment he swept to victory in Iowa's caucuses last January, Americans saw in Obama an inspiring message of unity and a remarkable, cool confidence — a trait they found particularly comforting when the U.S. economy tumbled.

Whether you voted for him or not, no one can deny the significance of this moment — when our audacious ideal was given new life.

— Henry J. Cordes
World-Herald Staff Writer

Obama promises honesty as he views the tough road ahead. Page 1W

Voters energized

Voters in Nebraska and across the nation surged to the polls in historic numbers, creating lines snaking out of polling places but producing few complaints. Page 1W

On Omaha.com:
■ Continual updates of election results; video of Obama and McCain's speeches Tuesday night
■ Full text of Obama's speech

INSIDE: 16-page special section

Featuring a two-page spread breaking down how Barack Obama won the presidential race, plus:
■ In-depth coverage of Nebraska and Iowa races, including a table of voting results;
■ House, Senate and governor races across the nation;
■ Photo pages profiling the Democratic and Republican presidential campaigns and the election scene Tuesday across the country

Midlands reaction

Emotions ran strong in Nebraska and Iowa as it became clear Tuesday night that Obama would win the presidency. Obama supporters savor their win while McCain backers hope their worst fears don't come true. Page 7W

37

When early voting ballots were tallied later in November, the World-Herald *reported that for the first time, the state had split its five electoral votes, giving one to Obama. No Democrat had won any since 1964.*

LOCALLY OWNED AND INDEPENDENT | WEDNESDAY, NOVEMBER 5, 2008   LASVEGASSUN.COM

LAS VEGAS SUN

2008 ELECTION EDITION

OBAMA MAKES HISTORY

CONGRESS: Dina Titus defeats Rep. Jon Porter. Shelley Berkley and Dean Heller reelected.

STATE SENATE: 2 Republicans from Vegas ousted. Dems control Senate for first time in 17 years.

PROPOSITIONS: Voters advise raising the hotel room tax to avoid cutting funding for education.

HOW HE WON NEVADA

President-elect Barack Obama greets supporters who packed Chicago's Grant Park on Tuesday night.
OZIER MUHAMMAD/ NEW YORK TIMES

THE TALLY

52%
POPULAR VOTE

HIS THREE KEYS: A candidate who effectively spoke to new voters and to black and Hispanic and working-class voters; a toxic political environment for Republicans; and organizational prowess developed over months.

By J. PATRICK COOLICAN AND MICHAEL J. MISHAK, *Las Vegas Sun*

This thing was over before it started.

Barack Obama won Nevada three weeks ago.

Not literally of course, but in mid-October the campaign's chief Nevada strategist, Rob Hill, and a few field operatives led a meeting of about 200 volunteer precinct captains at Elaine Wynn Elementary School. It was one of six such meetings held by Obama forces that night throughout the state.

Dedicated volunteers, by this point almost martial in their discipline and who themselves had recruited dozens of helpers, got their marching orders for the early voting program that would begin within days.

For months the campaign had been registering voters. When Hill arrived during the summer, the 100 paid organizers had a goal of signing up 70 to 100 new voters a week. But they kept blowing through those numbers.

He upped it to 200.

Veteran Northern Nevada Democrats were amazed at the registration advantage.

In the run-up to the January caucus, they were thrilled. But then, to their surprise, it continued.

"I've been astonished it hasn't leveled off," said Assemblywoman   *[See Obama, Page 8]*

Titus scores a personal comeback

After losing '06 governor's race, she beats incumbent in House

BY MICHAEL J. MISHAK AND J. PATRICK COOLICAN
Las Vegas Sun

After Dina Titus lost the 2006 governor's race to Jim Gibbons, who'd been accused of assaulting a women and other ethical misdeeds, she seemed to have lost some faith in politics.

She had been outspent 2-to-1 and pummeled with negative ads, and despite a Democratic wave across the country, she drew just 44 percent of the vote. She lashed out at rural voters, and her political future seemed uncertain, at best. Fellow Democrats saw her as a divisive figure.

Yet when a Democratic candidate for the Third Congressional District suddenly dropped out of the race this year, Democrats wooed her to take on Rep. Jon Porter.

This time, she ran a careful and disciplined campaign, listened to seasoned advisers and rode the Democratic wave, helped along by ample Democratic money from outside the state.

The campaign wasn't much, really, and in fact it seems she won far fewer votes than

[See Titus, Page 2]

DISTRICT 3

DINA TITUS
47%
OF THE VOTE

THE KEY:
She rides the Democratic wave and makes no unforced errors.

SAM MORRIS / LAS VEGAS SUN

State Sen. and now Congresswoman-elect Dina Titus greets supporters at the Nevada State Democratic Party election night party Tuesday at the Rio.

In barbershop, anxiety as results roll in

BY MIKE TRASK
Las Vegas Sun

Darryl Jones, a tall, quiet 35-year-old barber, arrived at work Tuesday to find an Obama flier hanging on the front door of his shop.

He had voted.

For Barack Obama.

So at 8:30 a.m. he begins cutting the hair on the first of 20 heads at Executive Cuts Barber Shop, on West Owens Avenue in a largely black area of Las Vegas. His customers, continuing a trend that has lasted for months, want to talk politics.

With his soft demeanor and backward brown hat, Jones moves effortlessly around one of the six black leather chairs, holding the clippers delicately with his fingertips, taking in the chatter. His 11-year-old son Darryl Jr. sits watching, waiting his turn for a haircut on this most important of days.

Nothing is off limits. Customers, many who have been going to his shop for nearly 20 years, talk race, religion, gas prices and, sometimes most passionately, NFL football.

[See Barber shop, Page 5]

LEILA NAVIDI / LAS VEGAS SUN

Timaree Elder gets his hair cut by Darryl Jones at a Las Vegas barbershop as a TV shows election coverage. In the weeks leading up to Tuesday's election, politics dominated discussion at the shop, in a largely black area.

TODAY'S SPECIAL EDITION

Sports and arts and entertainment sections will return Thursday. The comics and puzzles are on **Page 2.**

TWO REPUBLICAN STALWARTS FALL IN STATE SENATE

With the defeat of Sens. Joe Heck and Bob Beers comes Democratic control of the upper chamber and more power for Southern Nevada. **Page 3**

HOUR BY HOUR REPORTING ON HISTORIC DAY

The Sun follows campaign workers and the state's election chief as they pour selves into long, emotional election finale. **Page 6.**

Reid begins to relax as Senate race results show gains for Dems

BY LISA MASCARO
Sun Washington Bureau

WASHINGTON — Election night has just begun, and Senate Majority Leader Harry Reid is on the edge of his seat.

At a hotel suite not far from the Capitol, as Democrats are partying below, Reid is at the foot of the bed, staring at the TV.

Aides poke in and out of the room as he watches not only to see whether Sen. Barack Obama will be elected president but whether the Senate will gain enough Democrats to create a coveted 60-seat majority that could overcome Republican obstruction.

But it is too early in the night to make history.

So Reid talks on the phone with aides in Nevada, who update him on turnout in Clark County and northern Nevada. He asks about the weather in Elko.

[See Senate, Page 3]

THE TALLY

56
SEATS WON

+5
TOTAL GAIN

LAS VEGAS SUN EXCLUSIVE ONLINE COVERAGE   www.lasvegassun.com

VIEW: Photos of voters and the candidates from throughout Election Day.

READ: Stories, blogs and results from important local, state and national contests.

LISTEN: Clips from interviews with three key players in this year's election.

WATCH: Video of Obama and Dina Titus as their campaigns come to an end.

ELECTION 2008

CONCORD MONITOR

WEDNESDAY, NOVEMBER 5, 2008   concordmonitor.com   CONCORD, NEW HAMPSHIRE   50¢

| Lynch wins third term with landslide victory | Hodes and Shea-Porter will return to Congress | Shaheen takes Senate rematch against Sununu |

Obama makes history

President-elect leads Democratic sweep

Totals

PRESIDENT

	N.H.	U.S.
Percent reporting:	76%	77%
OBAMA (D):	**54%**	**51%**
McCAIN (R):	**45%**	**47%**

U.S. SENATE
Percent reporting: 76%

SHAHEEN (D): **52%**
SUNUNU (R): **45%**

CONGRESS

2nd DISTRICT
Percent reporting: 71%

HODES (D): **57%**
HORN (R): **41%**

1st DISTRICT
Percent reporting: 82%

SHEA-PORTER (D): **52%**
BRADLEY (R): **45%**

GOVERNOR
Percent reporting: 76%

LYNCH (D): **70%**
KENNEY (R): **28%**

N.H. HOUSE
MERRIMACK COUNTY
DISTRICT 12 (4 SEATS)

WALLNER (D): 3,663
RICE (D): 3,475
OSBORNE (D): 3,305
WATROUS (D): 3,005
KALB (R): 1,916
P. EAN (R): 1,727
INGRAM (R): 1,557
G. EAN (R): 1,436

EXECUTIVE COUNCIL
Percent reporting: 71%

SHEA (D): **54%**
ST. HILAIRE (R): **46%**

N.H. SENATE

7th DISTRICT
Percent reporting: 53%

JANEWAY (D): **51%**
SANBORN (R): **49%**

HOW AND WHY DID THEY VOTE?

It's not *just* the economy, stupid. Hundreds of New Hampshire voters interviewed by Monitor reporters at the polls yesterday were far more likely to cite the need for "change" than economic distress as their chief reason for supporting Barack Obama.

Those who voted for John McCain cited their own party loyalty, McCain's experience and character, or their distaste for Obama.

More than 500 voters in about two dozen towns were surveyed about the presidential race.

COMPLETE RESULTS
on pages B4 and B5

President-elect Barack Obama, a Democrat, celebrates during his rally in Chicago yesterday. Obama will be the first African American to serve as U.S. president.   AP

U.S. elects first black president

PAUL HODES wins Congress with wide lead. **B1**

CAROL SHEA-PORTER: "You did mean to send me to Washington." **B1**

JOHN LYNCH proves his popularity as governor. **B1**

DEMOCRATS appear in control of state Senate. **B1**

NEW HAMPSHIRE House results. **A5, A6**

CONCORD School Board has four newcomers. **B1**

KATHERINE ROGERS wins the race for Merrimack County attorney. **B3**

By MICHAEL D. SHEAR
and ROBERT BARNES
The Washington Post

Sen. Barack Obama of Illinois was elected the nation's 44th president yesterday, riding a reformist message of change and an inspirational exhortation of hope to become the first African American to ascend to the White House.

Obama, 47, the son of a Kenyan father and a white mother from Kansas, led a tide of Democratic victories across the nation in defeating Republican Sen. John McCain of Arizona, a 26-year veteran of Washington who could not overcome his connections to President Bush's increasingly unpopular administration.

"If there is anyone out there who still doubts that America is a place where all things are possible, who still wonders if the dream of our founders is alive in our time, who still questions the power of our

See **PRESIDENT – A8**

State rides leftward momentum

By FELICE BELMAN
Monitor staff

Not long ago, New Hampshire was among the most reliably Republican states in the nation – but no more. In a historic election amid extraordinary turnout, New Hampshire voted for Democrats up and down the election ballot yesterday.

New Hampshire chose Democrat Barack Obama for president over Republican John McCain.

Voters ousted one-term U.S. Sen. John Sununu, replacing him with Democrat Jeanne Shaheen, the former governor. Shaheen, who lost to Sununu in 2002, will be the state's first female senator and the first Democrat elected to the position since 1975.

The state also returned Democratic U.S. Reps. Paul Hodes and Carol Shea-Porter to Washington. Voters gave Democratic Gov. John Lynch a huge win. And at press time, Democrats appeared to have held on to their control of the state Senate and the Executive Council.

Locally, Democrat Katherine Rogers appeared victorious in her campaign for Merrimack County attorney.

When an exultant Ray Buck-

See **STATE – A8**

Shaheen claims Senate seat

By LAUREN R. DORGAN
Monitor staff

Democrat Jeanne Shaheen clinched a U.S. Senate race against incumbent Republican John Sununu on her second try last night, becoming the first New Hampshire woman ever elected to the Senate and the first Democratic senator elected from the state since 1975.

"Today, New Hampshire voters said they want a senator who will be a strong independent voice. New Hampshire voters said today they want a senator who will stand up to the special interests, a senator who will vote for middle class families," Shaheen, 61, a former three-term governor, told a cheering crowd in Manchester. "I am going to be that senator."

Six years ago, Shaheen, then

See **SHAHEEN – A8**

WILLIAMS DeSHAZER / Monitor staff

Former New Hampshire governor Jeanne Shaheen celebrates her defeat of U.S. Sen. John Sununu in Manchester last night.

CLOUDY
with sun.
High 62.
Low 43.
Courtney Cline, 6, of Franklin draws the day. **B8**

Classified	D2
Comics	C6
Editorial	B6
Food	D1
Local & State	B1
Neighbors	B3
Obituaries	B2
Sports	C1
Sudoku	D2
TV	D5

For daily delivery, call 224-4287 or 800-464-3415.

PEMBROKE ACADEMY
freshman and field hockey player dies after a car collision in Hooksett. **B2**

THE NEWSPAPER FOR NEW JERSEY

WEDNESDAY, NOVEMBER 5, 2008 / 50 CENTS

OBAMA REACHES THE MOUNTAINTOP

NATION PICKS FIRST AFRICAN-AMERICAN PRESIDENT

HUGE TURNOUT ALSO HELPS DEMOCRATS IN CONGRESS

40

The largest newspaper in New Jersey featured a headline evoking Dr. Martin Luther King Jr.'s last speech before he was assassinated.

President-elect Barack Obama arrives in Chicago's Grant Park with his wife, Michelle, and their daughters, Malia and Sasha, to deliver his victory speech to a huge hometown crowd early today.

SHAWN THEW/EUROPEAN PRESSPHOTO AGENCY

Economic crisis leads to decisive electoral win over McCain

BY J. SCOTT ORR STAR-LEDGER STAFF

Barack Obama's audacious presidential ambitions were realized yesterday as voters responded to his call for change with an overwhelming electoral victory that will make him the first African-American to ascend to the U.S. presidency.

Propelled by the passion of first-time voters, rank-and-file Democrats and minorities, the 47-year-old, first-term senator from Illinois easily defeated his vastly more experienced Republican opponent, John McCain, after a marathon 21-month campaign fought out at the previously uncharted nexus of politics and race.

"America can change. Our union can be perfected," Obama said in his victory speech early today to tens of thousands of supporters in Chicago.

In cobbling together his historic victory, Obama relied on wins in Pennsylvania and in states that were key to President Bush's victories in the last two elections — Ohio, Florida and Virginia. Obama's promise of hope and change resonated with voters who are facing the reality of an economy in turmoil. Predictably, New Jersey's 15

[See VICTORY, Page 11]

COMPLETE ELECTION COVERAGE INSIDE

■ Mark Di Ionno travels the state and finds a patchwork of passion and pride. **Page 5**

■ Republican Leonard Lance thumps Linda Stender in their congressional race. **Page 29**

■ Incumbent Democrat Frank Lautenberg easily defeats Dick Zimmer for U.S. Senate. **Page 29**

■ Find the latest election tallies and up-to-the-minute news at nj.com/elections.

95 Años CON DE LOS HISPANOS

EL DIARIO

1913-2008 **LA PRENSA** NUEVA YORK, MIERCOLES 5 DE NOVIEMBRE AÑO 2008

GOLDEN AWARD · THE JOSE MARTI PUBLISHING AWARDS

El Diario/LA PRENSA
Medalla de Oro
El mejor diario
Hispano de los
Estados Unidos
Asociación Nacional de Publicaciones Hispanas

WWW.ELDIARIONY.COM   50¢ (75¢ OUTSIDE NY & NJ)

PRESIDENTE

Histórica victoria
de Barack Obama
sobre John McCain
abre una nueva era
para los
Estados Unidos
—P2-8 y 24

Video: La esperanzas y los
temores de votantes latinos
www.impre.com/eldiariony

41

*The nation's oldest
Spanish-language
daily endorsed
Barack Obama,
citing his capacity
to restore confidence.
Nationally,
Hispanics voted for
Obama by a ratio of
more than 2-1.*

In the upper left corner, the newspaper referred readers to its Web site, which featured a large interactive map that displayed county-by-county results. On Election Day, nytimes.com had record-high traffic.

"All the News That's Fit to Print"

The New York Times

Late Edition

Today, limited sunshine, a shower, high 63. **Tonight,** cloudy, scattered showers, patchy fog, low 55. **Tomorrow,** rain ends, remaining cloudy, high 62. Weather map, Page B19.

VOL. CLVIII . . No. 54,485 + © 2008 The New York Times NEW YORK, WEDNESDAY, NOVEMBER 5, 2008 $5 beyond the greater New York metropolitan area. $1.50

OBAMA

RACIAL BARRIER FALLS IN DECISIVE VICTORY

08 ONLINE

- *The latest state-by-state results: the presidential contest and House, Senate and governors' races.*
- *The Caucus blog: updates from The Times's political staff.*

- *Interactive graphics: the electoral map, voter profiles and analysis.*
- *Video, audio and photos: reactions from the voters and the campaigns.*

nytimes.com

PRESIDENT-ELECT

THE LONG CAMPAIGN

Journey to the Top

The story of Senator Barack Obama's journey to the pinnacle of American politics is the story of a campaign that was, even in the view of many rivals, almost flawless. After a somewhat lackluster start, Mr. Obama and his team delivered. They developed a strategy to secure the nomination, and stuck with it even after setbacks. PAGE P1

SENATE

NORTH CAROLINA

Elizabeth Dole Is Out

After leading by a double-digit margin, the Republican Senator Elizabeth Dole, left, was defeated by State Senator Kay R. Hagan. In the campaign's final week, Mrs. Dole came under criticism for an advertisement that linked Ms. Hagan to a group called the Godless Americans. PAGE P12

VIRGINIA

Mark Warner Wins

Extending the Democrats' advantage in the Senate, former Gov. Mark R. Warner of Virginia easily won his race to replace John W. Warner (no relation), a retiring Republican. PAGE P12

NEW HAMPSHIRE

Sununu Is Defeated

Another leading Republican, Senator John E. Sununu, was ousted by a wide margin by Jeanne Shaheen, the former New Hampshire governor whom he beat in 2002. PAGE P12

HOUSE

CONNECTICUT

G.O.P. Stalwart Falls

Representative Christopher Shays, the last Republican House member from New England and a political Houdini who escaped previous Democratic attempts to topple him, was defeated by a political novice, Jim Himes. PAGE P15

NEW YORK

LEGISLATURE

Democrats Take Senate

Democrats won a majority in the New York State Senate, putting the party in control of both houses of the Legislature and the governor's office for the first time since the New Deal. Voters ousted two Republican senators whose combined years in office spanned more than half a century. PAGE P15

FOR HOME DELIVERY CALL 1-800-NYTIMES

DOUG MILLS/THE NEW YORK TIMES

President-elect Barack Obama with his wife, Michelle, and their daughters in Chicago on Tuesday night.

Democrats in Congress Strengthen Grip

By ADAM NAGOURNEY

Barack Hussein Obama was elected the 44th president of the United States on Tuesday, sweeping away the last racial barrier in American politics with ease as the country chose him as its first black chief executive.

The election of Mr. Obama amounted to a national catharsis — a repudiation of a historically unpopular Republican president and his economic and foreign policies, and an embrace of Mr. Obama's call for a change in the direction and the tone of the country.

But it was just as much a strikingly symbolic moment in the evolution of the nation's fraught racial history, a breakthrough that would have seemed unthinkable just two years ago.

Mr. Obama, 47, a first-term senator from Illinois, defeated Senator John McCain of Arizona, 72, a former prisoner of war who was making his second bid for the presidency.

To the very end, Mr. McCain's campaign was eclipsed by an opponent who was nothing short of a phenomenon, drawing huge crowds epitomized by the tens of thousands of people who turned out to hear Mr. Obama's victory speech in Grant Park in Chicago.

Mr. McCain also fought the headwinds of a relentlessly hostile political environment, weighted down with the baggage left to him by President Bush and an economic collapse that took place in the middle of the general election campaign.

"If there is anyone out there who still doubts that America is a place where all things are possible, who still wonders if the dream of our founders is alive in our time, who still questions the power of our democracy, tonight is your answer," said Mr. Obama, standing before a huge wooden lectern with a row of American flags at his back, casting his eyes to a crowd that stretched far into the Chicago night.

"It's been a long time coming," the president-elect added, "but tonight, because of what we did on this date in this election at this defining moment, change has come to America."

Mr. McCain delivered his concession speech under clear skies on the lush lawn of the Arizona Biltmore, in Phoenix, where he and his wife had held their wedding reception. The crowd reacted with scattered boos as he offered his congratulations to Mr. Obama and saluted the historical significance of the moment.

"This is a historic election, and I recognize the significance it has for African-Americans and for the special pride that must be theirs tonight," Mr. McCain said, adding, "We both realize that we have come a long way from the injustices that once stained our nation's reputation."

Not only did Mr. Obama capture the presidency, but he led his party to sharp gains in Congress. This puts

Continued on Page P3

THE CHALLENGE

No Time for Laurels; Now the Hard Part

By PETER BAKER

WASHINGTON — No president since before Barack Obama was born has ascended to the Oval Office confronted by the accumulation of seismic challenges awaiting him. Historians grasping for parallels point to Abraham Lincoln taking office as the nation was collapsing into Civil War, or Franklin D. Roosevelt arriving in Washington in the throes of the Great Depression.

The task facing Mr. Obama does not rise to those levels, but that these are the comparisons most often cited sobers even Democrats rejoicing at their return to power. On the shoulders of a 47-year-old first-term senator, with the power of inspiration yet no real executive experience, now falls the responsibility of prosecuting two wars, protecting the nation from terrorist threat and stitching back together a shredded economy.

Given the depth of these issues, Mr. Obama has little choice but to "put your arm around chaos," in the words of Leon E. Panetta, the former White House chief of staff who has been advising his transition team.

"You better damn well do the tough stuff up front, because if you think you can delay the tough decisions and tiptoe past the graveyard, you're in for a lot of trouble," Mr. Panetta said. "Make the decisions that involve pain and sacrifice up front."

What kind of decision maker and leader Mr. Obama will be remains unclear even to many of his supporters. Will he be willing to use his political capital and act boldly, or will he move cautiously and risk being paralyzed by competing demands from within his own party? His performance under the harsh lights of the campaign trail suggests a figure with remarkable coolness and confidence under enormous pressure, yet also one who rarely veers off the methodical path he lays out.

"It leads you to wonder whether passivity is the way he approaches most things," said John R. Bolton, President Bush's former ambassador to the United Na-

Continued on Page P4

THE MOMENT

After Decades, A Time to Reap

By KEVIN SACK

ALBANY, Ga. — Rutha Mae Harris backed her silver Town Car out of the driveway early Tuesday morning, pointed it toward her polling place on Mercer Avenue and started to sing.

"I'm going to vote like the spirit say vote," Miss Harris chanted softly.

I'm going to vote like the
spirit say vote,
I'm going to vote like the
spirit say vote,
And if the spirit say vote I'm
going to vote,
Oh Lord, I'm going to vote
when the spirit say vote.

As a 21-year-old student (on right in photo), she had bellowed that same freedom song at mass meetings at Mount Zion Baptist Church back in 1961, the year Barack Obama was born in Hawaii, a universe away. She sang it again while marching on Albany's City Hall, where she and other black students demanded the right to vote, and in the cramped and filthy cells of the city jail, which the Rev. Dr. Martin Luther King Jr. described as the worst he ever inhabited.

For those like Miss Harris who withstood jailings and beatings and threats to their livelihoods, all because they wanted to vote, the short drive to the polls on Tuesday culminated a lifelong journey from a time that is at once unrecognizable and eerily familiar here in southwest Georgia. As they exited the voting booths, some in wheelchairs, others with canes, these foot soldiers of the civil rights movement could not suppress either their jubilation or their astonishment at having voted for an African-American for president of the United States.

"They didn't give us our mule and our acre, but things are better," Miss Harris, 67, said with a gratified smile. "It's time to reap some of the harvest."

When Miss Harris arrived at the city gymnasium where she votes, her 80-year-old friend Mamie L. Nelson greeted her with a hug. "We marched, we sang and now it's happening," Ms. Nelson said. "It's really a feeling I

Continued on Page P6

THE PROMISE

For Many Abroad, An Ideal Renewed

By ETHAN BRONNER

GAZA — From far away, this is how it looks: There is a country out there where tens of millions of white Christians, voting freely, select as their leader a black man of modest origin, the son of a Muslim. There is a place on Earth — call it America — where such a thing happens.

Even where the United States is held in special contempt, like here in this benighted Palestinian coastal strip, the "glorious epic of Barack Obama," as the leftist French editor Jean Daniel calls it, makes America — the idea as much as the actual place — stand again, perhaps only fleetingly, for limitless possibility.

"It allows us all to dream a little," said Oswaldo Calvo, 58, a Venezuelan political activist in Caracas, in a comment echoed to correspondents of The New York Times on four continents in the days leading up to the election.

Tristram Hunt, a British historian, put it this way: Mr. Obama "brings the narrative that everyone wants to return to — that America is the land of extraordinary opportunity and possibility, where miracles happen."

But wonder is almost overwhelmed by relief. Mr. Obama's election offers most non-Americans a sense that the imperial power capable of doing such good and such harm — a country that, they complain, preached justice but tortured its captives, launched a disastrous war in Iraq, turned its back on the environment and greedily dragged the world into economic chaos — saw the errors of its ways over the past eight years and shifted course.

They say the country that weakened democratic forces abroad through a tireless but often ineffective campaign for democracy — dismissing results it found unsavory, cutting deals with dictators it needed as allies in its other battles — was now shining a transformative beacon with its own democratic exercise.

It would be hard to overstate how fervently vast

Continued on Page P4

ASSEMBLY
Four incumbents sail to victory:
Hyer-Spencer, Titone, Tobacco, Cusick
PAGE E 9

CONGRESS
McMahon defeats Straniere,
returning seat to the Democrats.
PAGE E 5

STATE SENATE
Two incumbents win re-election:
Lanza and Savino
PAGE E 9

Staten Island Advance

SPECIAL EDITION | DECISION 2008

BREAKING NEWS ALL DAY ON SILIVE.COM

WEDNESDAY, NOVEMBER 5, 2008

PUBLISHED SINCE 1886 | 50 CENTS

Barack Obama
will be our 44th.
And our first.

AMERICA'S

43

*On November 4,
Staten Island was
an island in another
respect: It was the
only borough of New
York City that voted
in favor of McCain.*

HISTORIC
VOTE

■ **A PASSIONATE OBAMA**
"America, I have never been more hopeful
than I am tonight," the president-elect
declares in an eloquent victory speech. **E 3**

■ **A GRACIOUS McCAIN**
"These are difficult times," Sen. John McCain
tells supporters in his concession speech,
pledging to help the Democratic victor. **E 3**

■ **A CELEBRATION ON STATEN ISLAND**
McCain won this borough 52-48. But Obama
revelers in Clifton are too busy looking
at the big picture to even care. **E 2**

8 31107 00800 8

NOVEMBER 12–18, 2008 **I** VOL. LIII NO. 46 **I** AMERICA'S LARGEST WEEKLY NEWSPAPER

VILLAGEVOICE.COM **I** FREE

ENEMY OF MY ENEMY: DWOSKIN
ON THE INSANITY OF ASYLUM

MUSTO GOES ONE-ON-ONE
WITH PARIS HILTON

the village VOICE

44

*Tom Robbins
reported from
Lorain, Ohio, a
northern industrial
town hit hard by
plant closings and
home foreclosures—
economic issues
Obama pledged to
address.*

A REPORT FROM A
RUST-BUCKET TOWN
**THE GREAT
BLACK
HOPE**
BY TOM ROBBINS

WEDNESDAY ■ NOVEMBER 5, 2008 ■ 50¢

Interactive election maps @ charlotteobserver.com

13 PAGES OF ELECTION COVERAGE

The Charlotte Observer

'Change has come to America'

Barack Obama elected as nation's first African American president. **6A**

"If there is anyone out there who still doubts America is a place where all things are possible ... tonight is your answer," President-elect Barack Obama said Tuesday night, after taking the stage with daughters Sasha (left) and Malia and his wife, Michelle. Sen. John McCain said earlier, "His success alone commands my respect." DANIEL ACKER - BLOOMBERG NEWS PHOTO

N.C. Governor

1st woman wins post: Perdue beats McCrory

Bev Perdue celebrates her win Tuesday, capping a 22-year career in state government.

SARA D. DAVIS – ASSOCIATED PRESS PHOTO

Lt. Gov. Bev Perdue, a Democrat, narrowly defeated Charlotte Mayor Pat McCrory Tuesday, extending 16 years of Democratic control of the N.C. governor's office. McCrory, a Republican, was trailing early today in Mecklenburg, his home county. **14A.**

Election Inside

■ **MECKLENBURG COUNTY COMMISSIONERS:** Democrats widened their majority on the Mecklenburg Board of County Commissioners, sweeping all three at-large seats. **17A**

■ **LOCAL BONDS:** Voters appeared likely to pass $477 million in bonds Tuesday that will allow for a range of civic projects, including affordable housing and improvements to roads. **17A**

■ **HOW DID WE VOTE?:** See Mecklenburg County results. **10A**

Senate

Hagan defeats Dole to take Senate seat

Democrat Kay Hagan of Greensboro defeated incumbent U.S. Sen. Elizabeth Dole Tuesday night, ending a campaign that featured millions of dollars of highly personal attack advertising. The defeat probably marked the end of Dole's long political career. **12A**

TED RICHARDSON – (RALEIGH) NEWS & OBSERVER
Democrat Kay Hagan won an upset unthinkable a year ago.

 66° 46°

Cloudy, warmer: Mostly cloudy but a little warmer this afternoon. Clearing overnight, then sunny Thursday with highs in the 70s. **8B**

Ask Amy 9E
Business 1D
Classified 6C
Comics 8E

Editorial 20A
Horoscope 8E
Movies 7E
Obituaries 6B

Sports 1C
TV 7E
Delivery Assistance or to Subscribe
800-532-5350

45

Siding with Barack Obama by a slim margin, North Carolinians also voted in Beverly Perdue, the state's first female governor.

IN TRIANGLE&CO: WAKE BOARD TILTS DEMOCRATIC ... DEMS GAIN IN STATE COUNCIL ... N.C. HOUSE RACES TIGHT

THE NEWS&OBSERVER

NEWS UPDATES AT WWW.NEWSOBSERVER.COM • FINAL EDITION, 50 CENTS   WEDNESDAY, NOVEMBER 5, 2008   ©2008 THE NEWS AND OBSERVER PUBLISHING COMPANY • RALEIGH, N.C.

★ ★ ★ ★ ★ **11 PAGES OF ELECTION 2008 COVERAGE** ★ ★ ★ ★ ★

OBAMA WINS

A RACIAL BARRIER FALLS AS AMERICA ELECTS ITS FIRST BLACK PRESIDENT
'LET US SUMMON A NEW SPIRIT' ★ N.C. LEANS TO FIRST DEMOCRAT SINCE 1976

HAGAN TAKES DOLE'S SENATE SEAT

PERDUE TO BE FIRST FEMALE N.C. GOVERNOR

AFP/GETTY IMAGES PHOTO BY EMMANUEL DUNAND

Barack Obama, the Democratic senator from Illinois, stepped into history Tuesday, becoming the first black man elected to the nation's highest office. He won the hard-fought race by out-organizing his opponent, Arizona Sen. John McCain, surpassing his rival in fundraising and getting far more volunteers on the ground in crucial states. Obama also benefited from a political climate that heavily favored Democrats — an economic meltdown that took place under the watch of an unpopular Republican president. See story, **Page 7A.**

★ ★ ★ **ELECTION COVERAGE: PAGES 7A-13A AND 1B-4B** ★ ★ ★

WEATHER

TODAY: Mostly cloudy with some morning rain. High 63, low 50.
THURSDAY: Partly cloudy skies and breezy. High 70, low 47. **16B**

INDEX

Business .....9B   Editorials 14A
Classified ....13D   Films 9D
Comics ......10D   Puzzles 2D
Deaths ....14B   TV 8D

A B

U.S. SENATE

STAFF PHOTO BY TED RICHARDSON

HARDLY KNOWN A YEAR AGO, HAGAN STUNS DOLE

In a result that would have been virtually unthinkable, Democrat Kay Hagan defeated Sen. Elizabeth Dole. With 95 of 100 counties reporting, Hagan led Dole by 52.5 percent to 44.4 percent. **10A**

GOVERNOR

STAFF PHOTO BY ETHAN HYMAN

PERDUE WINS A TIGHT RACE WITH McCRORY

Lt. Gov. Beverly Perdue defeated Charlotte Mayor Pat McCrory to become the state's first female governor. The slumping economy will challenge Perdue and hamper her efforts to enact new initiatives. **13A**

Obama's updraft lifts N.C. Democrats

North Carolina, long one of the most contested pieces of political turf in America, was trending blue Tuesday as Democrats rode uncertainty about the economy and the Iraq war to a strong showing.

Sen. Barack Obama, a black man from Chicago, was running a more competitive race than any Democrat since Bill Clinton in 1992 — locked in a tough contest with Republican Sen. John McCain.

Rob Christensen

Obama's powerful and well-financed grass-roots organization helped lift Democrat Kay Hagan to the U.S. Senate and Beverly Perdue to the governor's office.

The Obama effect also fueled a strong Democratic showing up and down the ballot, with the Democrats retaining control of the legislature and picking up a congressional seat.

"The last time the Democrats pulled the hat trick was 1960," when Gov. Terry Sanford, Sen. B. Everett Jordan and President Kennedy won, said Gary Pearce, a long-time Democratic strategist. Whether Obama wins North Car-

SEE **CHRISTENSEN**, PAGE 13A

THE BG NEWS

ESTABLISHED 1920
A daily independent student press serving
the campus and surrounding community

Volume 103 , Issue 53   **Wednesday,** November 5, 2008   www.bgnews.com

OBAMA WINS PRESIDENCY

By David Espo
The Associated Press

WASHINGTON — Barack Obama swept to victory as the nation's first black president last night in an electoral college landslide that overcame racial barriers as old as America itself. "Change has come," he told a huge throng of jubilant supporters.

The son of a black father from Kenya and a white mother from Kansas, the Democratic senator from Illinois sealed his historic triumph by defeating Republican Sen. John McCain in a string of wins in hard-fought battleground states — Ohio, Florida, Iowa and more. He captured Virginia, too, the first candidate of his party in 40 years to do so.

On a night for Democrats to savor, they not only elected Obama the nation's 44th president but padded their majorities in the House and Senate, and in January will control both the White House and Congress for the first time since 1994.

A survey of voters leaving polling places showed the economy was by far the top Election Day issue. Six in 10 voters said so, and none of the other top issues — energy, Iraq, terrorism and health care — was picked by more than one in 10.

Obama's election capped a meteoric rise — from mere state senator to president-elect in four years.

Spontaneous celebrations erupted from Atlanta to New York and Philadelphia as word of Obama's victory spread. A big crowd filled Pennsylvania Avenue in front of the White House.

In his first speech as victor, to more than 100,000 supporters at Grant Park in his home town of Chicago, Obama catalogued the challenges ahead. "The greatest of a lifetime," he said, "two wars, a planet in peril, the worst financial crisis in a century."

He added, "There are many who won't agree with every decision or policy I make as president, and we know that government can't solve every problem. But I will always be honest with

See **OBAMA** | Page 2

ENOCH WU | THE BG NEWS

LIVING HISTORY, FEELING GOOD: Around 300 students crowded the Union last night to celebrate Barack Obama clenching the presidency. As he delivered his victory speech live from Chicago, the crowd of mostly black students in the Union cheered and danced in celebration. "Gobama, victory! I'm living history!" shouted Black Student Union historian Dean Bryson. He was focused especially on Obama's reference to the 106-year-old black woman who waited her whole life to see an African-American in office. "She's all I've been thinking about all day." While Obama's victory was especially meaningful for the black community, Nim Igumbor, a graduate student from Kenya, said all of America should be proud of the "realization of a dream."

When Ohio was called for Obama, the editor and photo editor ran to the student union to capture campus reaction. The campaign buttons show winners of local elections.

City Republicans celebrate local wins, lament national losses

By Tim Sampson
Executive Editor

Despite major Republican losses in the presidential election and in Senate and House races across the country, incumbent GOP officials in Wood County managed a near sweep in yesterday's election.

Locally, Republicans won races in the U.S. House and Senate, the State House and Senate, county sheriff and clerk of courts. The only local seat won by a Democrat was one of two county commissioner races where 24-year incumbent Alvin L. Perkins kept his seat.

The sharp contrast between national and local results made for a mixed mood at the Republican watch party held at the Stone Ridge Country Club in Bowling Green last night. Attendees were celebrating the victories of friends and colleagues while commiserating Barack Obama's substantial victory over John McCain.

Although many in attendance knew that McCain's chances were narrow going into yesterday's election, many were choosing to hold out hope until all the votes were tallied.

See **GOP** | Page 2

Local Democrats cheer on Obama's presidential win

By Kristen Vasas
City Editor

On the night of one of the most historic elections in America's history, the Wood County Democrats and an assortment of Bowling Green citizens gathered to cheer on their hope for change in the future: President-elect Barack Obama.

With roughly 100 participants gathered in the Bowling Green Country Club, Democratic supporters ranging in age from six to 91 met to watch the results of the election pour in from across the United States.

"We've had eight years of pretty miserable rule, and we've been through periods where we've had pretty tough times," Wood County Democratic Party Chair Mike Zickar said. "Our change is finally here and I think we're ready for it."

With the Illinois senator sweeping not only Wood County, but the state of Ohio, democratic supporters unanimously agreed that no other candidate would be able to handle the critical issues facing America, including the failing economy, the Iraq War and the national deficit.

See **DEMS** | Page 2

OHIO BALLOT RESULTS:

YES ☒ NO ☐	YES ☒ NO ☐	YES ☒ NO ☐	YES ☒ NO ☐	YES ☐ NO ☒
ISSUE 1	**ISSUE 2**	**ISSUE 3**	**ISSUE 5**	**ISSUE 6**
Proposed Constitutional Amendment to provide for earlier filing deadlines for statewide ballot issues	Proposed Constitutional Amendment to authorize the state to issue bonds to continue the Clean Ohio program for environmental revitalization and conservation.	Proposed Constitutional Amendment to protect private property rights in ground water, lakes and other waterways	Referendum on legislation making changes to check cashing lending, sometimes known as "payday lending," fees, interest rates and practices	Proposed Constitutional Amendment by initiative petition for a casino near Wilmington in Southwest Ohio and distribute tax monies from the casino to all Ohio counties

WWW.OHIOMEANSBUSINESS.COM

CAMPUS	**FORUM**	**SPORTS**	**PEOPLE ON THE STREET**
Party at the Pub	**Republicans, don't go to Canada**	**Back on the court**	How long did you wait to vote?
Both Republicans and Democrats filled the Black Swamp Pub last night to watch the election unfold as votes were tallied on national television | **Page 3**	Many political die-hards said they'd move to Canada if their candidate didn't win, but Executive Editor Tim Sampson declares that all is not lost, and the choice to expatriate would be negative for the country | **Page 4**	The lady Falcons defeated the University of Findlay, 90-59, in a home opening exhibition game | **Page 6**	**KEVIN NOVAK** Freshman, Sports Management "Half hour." | **Page 4**

▷ **VISIT BGNEWS.COM:** NEWS, SPORTS, UPDATES, MULTIMEDIA AND FORUMS FOR YOUR EVERYDAY LIFE

The Columbus Dispatch

High 74 | Low 48
Details B14

WWW.DISPATCH.COM

50 CENTS
75 cents in select areas outside Franklin County.

WEDNESDAY, NOVEMBER 5, 2008

OBAMA MAKES HISTORY

AMERICA ELECTS ITS FIRST BLACK PRESIDENT

OHIO, OTHER MAJOR STATES GO FOR DEMOCRAT

48

Ohio voters have picked the winning presidential candidate in the last twelve elections, including this one.

JEWEL SAMAD | AFP/GETTY IMAGES

Sen. Barack Obama and his family join the raucous victory celebration in Chicago's Grant Park. The senator from Illinois completed a two-year campaign with an overwhelming victory.

Win restores blacks' faith

Thousands celebrate what they thought they would never see

By Alan Johnson
THE COLUMBUS DISPATCH

When she prayed in the past few weeks, 87-year-old Florence Blake asked God to let her live long enough to see Barack Obama's election.

"Then I'll be ready to go home," the Worthington woman said.

She made it.

For Blake and thousands of other black Ohioans, Obama's election yesterday to the most powerful office in the world is something they never expected to see in their lifetimes — maybe even their children's lifetimes.

"It's a miracle," said Ed Willis, 82, who was principal of East High School for 15 years. "He's a special person. No one could have done it except him."

Many consider it vindication and victory after 200 years of slavery, oppression and prejudice, sitting at the back of the bus, attending separate schools, facing discrimination for jobs

See **BLACKS** Page A4

DORAL CHENOWETH III | DISPATCH

Willie Lewis-Slade, left, and William Farrar celebrate the announcement of Barack Obama winning Ohio and the presidency during a victory party last night Downtown at Club Ice.

Call for new politics a winning appeal

By Joe Hallett
THE COLUMBUS DISPATCH

▶ Analysis | A3
▶ Obama's win celebrated by people across Africa | A5

In the nation's 233rd year, Democrat Barack Obama became the first black person elected to the White House, unshackling from the restraints of racism the American dream that anyone can grow up to be president.

The 47-year-old Hawaiian-born son of a father from Kenya and mother from Kansas swept to a resounding national victory last night, frustrating Republican rival John McCain's bid for one more storied political comeback.

Minutes after Obama won traditionally Republican Virginia, television networks announced shortly after 11

p.m. that he had surpassed the needed 270 electoral votes, sparking pandemonium in Chicago's Grant Park, where thousands waited to hear from the president-elect.

Obama, appearing on stage with his wife, Michelle, and their two daughters, seized the moment: "If there is anyone out there who still doubts that America is a place where all things are possible; who still wonders if the dream of our founders is alive in our time; who still questions the power of our democracy, tonight is your answer."

The election of Obama and

his running mate, Sen. Joe Biden of Delaware, culminated a historic presidential race that captivated the attention of the nation and world for the better part of two years.

Obama ran a disciplined campaign, unwavering from his call for a new kind of cooperative politics. His message appealed across the racial divide and proffered Obama as a transcendent agent of change in the mold of the late Robert F. Kennedy.

"What began 21 months ago in the depths of winter must not end on this autumn night," he told the Grant Park audience. "This victory alone is not the change we seek — it is only the chance for us to

See **VICTORY** Page A4

THE DAY AT THE POLLS

Voting problems? Not in Ohio

Difficulties mostly minor despite huge turnout

By Mark Niquette
THE COLUMBUS DISPATCH

Sunny skies yesterday were a stark contrast to the dreary Election Day four years ago. And despite some gloomy predictions, problems that plagued the 2004 presidential election in Ohio did not materialize this year.

Lines swelled early in the day and at other peak voting hours in many places, and there were minor glitches and confusion about provisional ballots.

But there were no last-minute lawsuits to keep the polls open and no major controversies like those that made the Buckeye State the poster child for election

See **VOTING** Page A5

V★TE 2008

DISPATCH.COM
Go online for the latest vote tallies and all the overnight developments.

KEY ELECTION OUTCOMES

U.S. HOUSE: Austria, Tiberi win, **A3**
CASINOS: Voters say no again, **B1**
PAYDAY LENDING: High interest rejected, **B1**
ATTORNEY GENERAL: Cordray romps, **B1**
COLUMBUS SCHOOLS LEVY: Passes, **B1**
COLUMBUS BOND PACKAGE: All six pass, **B4**
JUDGESHIPS: Belskis ousted, **B4**

WWW.TULSAWORLD.COM
WEDNESDAY
NOVEMBER 5, 2008

Tulsa World

■ LOCALLY OWNED SINCE 1905 ■

FINAL HOME EDITION

75¢

✓ **Sen. Barack Obama, (D) 51.4%**
Popular vote: 56,330,299 Okla. vote: 492,138

Sen. John McCain, (R) 47.2%
Popular vote: 51,294,061 Okla. vote: 936,100

YES HE DID

President-elect Barack Obama waves to the crowd after giving his victory speech at Grant Park in Chicago on Tuesday night. PABLO MARTINEZ MONSIVAIS/Associated Press

Obama's triumph is historic moment

BY DAVID ESPO
Associated Press

WASHINGTON — Barack Obama swept to victory as the country's first black president Tuesday night in an Electoral College landslide that overcame racial barriers as old as the United States itself.

"Change has come," he told a jubilant hometown Chicago crowd estimated at nearly a quarter-million people.

The son of a black father from Kenya and a white mother from Kansas, the Democratic senator from Illinois sealed his historic triumph by defeating Sen. John McCain, the Republican nominee, in a string of victories in hard-fought battleground states — Ohio, Florida, Iowa and more. He captured Virginia, too, making him the first candidate of his party in 44 years to do so.

On a night for Democrats to savor, they not only elected Obama as the 44th president but padded their majorities in the House and Senate. In January, they will control both the White House and Congress for the first time since 1994.

John McCain

A survey of voters leaving polling places showed that the economy was by far the top Election Day issue. Six in 10 voters said so, and none of the other top issues — energy, Iraq, terrorism and health care — was picked by more than one in 10.

Obama's election capped a meteoric rise — from mere state senator to president-elect in four years.

Spontaneous celebrations erupted from Atlanta to New York and Philadelphia as word of Obama's victory spread. A big crowd filled Pennsylvania Avenue in front of the White House.

In his first speech as the victor, to an enor-

SEE **OBAMA** EE8

PRESIDENTIAL REACTION

Locals gleeful or dismayed

BY DENVER NICKS
World Staff Writer

Tulsans reacted with a range of emotions — from unbridled glee to disappointment to cautious optimism — to news that the United States had elected its first black president.

"I feel real good. You know the way I feel? Yeeea!" said Jacqueline Embray, leaping into the air at a watch party at the Greenwood Cultural Center.

"Tonight is a call to celebration," said Toni Wynes. "I'm so happy, I could fly. The dream has come true."

"I'm just thrilled to be on the same ballot (as Obama)," said Sally Frasier, an elector for the president-elect from Oklahoma.

"I'm sorry that I won't get to use my elector status in the state of Oklahoma, but I'm sure excited about the national scene, the U.S. Senate and the president's race," said Frasier.

SEE **LOCALS** EE8

CITY OF TULSA STREETS PACKAGE

Voters OK streets plan

BY BRIAN BARBER AND P.J. LASSEK
World Staff Writers

Tulsa voters paved the way Tuesday for the city to spend $451.6 million to fix the cracked and crumbling streets.

Both propositions that will provide funding for the five-year tax program were easily approved.

Proposition 1 — the sales tax portion — captured 61 percent of the votes and proposition 2 — the property tax portion — got 60 percent of the votes with 219 of 219 precincts reporting.

"We listened carefully to what the citizens wanted and that's what we put on the ballot," Mayor Kathy Taylor said after proclaiming victory at a watch party at the Tulsa Press Club.

Councilor G.T. Bynum, who pushed this pared-down program over a $2 billion, 12-year version, said voters approved it, even in tough economic times, because the

SEE **FIX** EE6

Election 2008

Democrats expand on control of U.S. Senate. **3**

See full U.S. Senate and U.S. House results and a map	Inhofe wins third full term in U.S. Senate.	John Sullivan, Dan Boren easily retain seats. ✓Sullivan 66% Olliver 34% ✓Boren 70% Wickson 30%	See a state-by-state breakdown of voting results	Riley falls in state Senate District 37; GOP takes control ✓Newberry 63% Riley 37%	In HD 71, Republican Dan Sullivan beats George Bullock ✓Sullivan 54% Bullock 46%	Karen Keith wins District 2 County Commission post ✓Keith 53% Bell 47%	Voters approve four state questions by large margins.
2	**3**	**3**	**4**	**5**	**5**	**6**	**7**

  ONLINE
See the official results of Tuesday's election.
tulsaworld.com

Daily - 75 cents

49

This headline was one of many that played on Obama's campaign slogan of "Yes, we can," though in this state, he couldn't—McCain won every county.

MERKLEY CLINGS TO SLIM LEAD | A11

50

Some papers approached the front-page design as a poster, anticipating that people would want to save it.

WEDNESDAY • NOVEMBER 5, 2008

PORTLAND, OREGON • **SUNRISE EDITION**

The Oregonian

OREGONLIVE.COM/POLITICS

OBAMA'S TIME
America votes for historic change | A11

COMPREHENSIVE ELECTION COVERAGE | A11-20, B1-5

DOUG MILLS/THE NEW YORK TIMES

Copyright © 2008, Oregonian Publishing Co.
Vol. 158, No. 53,223, 56 pages

7   14170 00043   1

Key results **For a complete list, see A11**

Big gains in Congress
Democrats scored some convincing victories in both chambers, picking up Senate seats in North Carolina, New Hampshire and Virginia | **A18**

Crime measure wins
The Oregon Legislature's less-costly alternative to Kevin Mannix's anti-crime initiative will go into effect, but a slew of other measures fail | **A19**

Elephants win: Zoo bond passes
Portland-area voters approve a $125 million bond measure that would provide more space and more natural surroundings for the Oregon Zoo's elephants, polar bears, chimps and other animals | **B1**

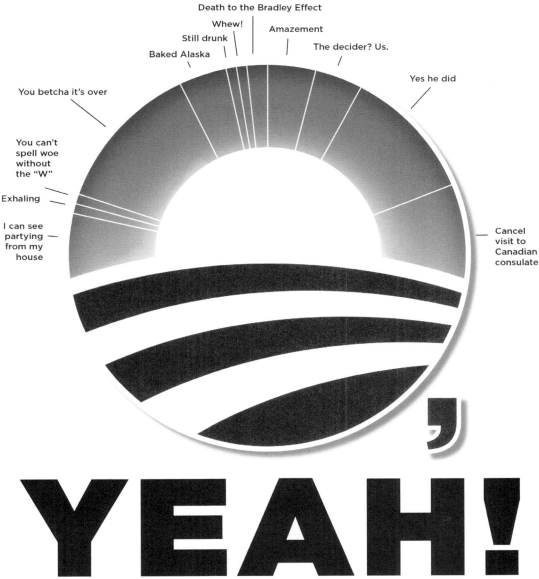

WILLAMETTE WEEK PORTLAND'S NEWSWEEKLY

Death to the Bradley Effect

Whew!

Still drunk

Amazement

Baked Alaska

The decider? Us.

You betcha it's over

Yes he did

You can't spell woe without the "W"

Exhaling

I can see partying from my house

Cancel visit to Canadian consulate

'YEAH!

AMERICA COMES TO ITS SENSES.

"YANKING OUT THE SIGNS AND RUNNING LIKE A SCARED RABBIT..." P. 13

WWEEK.COM
VOL 34/52
10.05.2008

51

This alternative newspaper used Obama's campaign logo to suggest a pie chart that showed excitement about the election.

52

Obama won this "battleground" state by a healthy margin, like the four Democratic presidential candidates who preceded him.

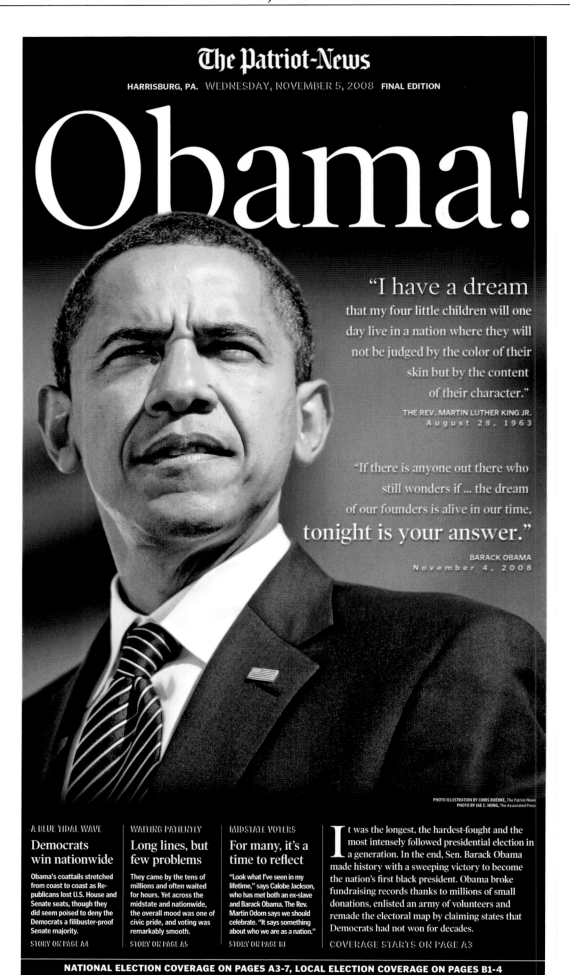

The Patriot-News

HARRISBURG, PA. WEDNESDAY, NOVEMBER 5, 2008 **FINAL EDITION**

Obama!

"I have a dream that my four little children will one day live in a nation where they will not be judged by the color of their skin but by the content of their character."

THE REV. MARTIN LUTHER KING JR.
August 28, 1963

"If there is anyone out there who still wonders if ... the dream of our founders is alive in our time, tonight is your answer."

BARACK OBAMA
November 4, 2008

PHOTO ILLUSTRATION BY CHRIS BOEHKE, The Patriot-News
PHOTO BY JAE C. HONG, The Associated Press

A BLUE TIDAL WAVE

Democrats win nationwide

Obama's coattails stretched from coast to coast as Republicans lost U.S. House and Senate seats, though they did seem poised to deny the Democrats a filibuster-proof Senate majority.

STORY ON PAGE A4

WAITING PATIENTLY

Long lines, but few problems

They came by the tens of millions and often waited for hours. Yet across the midstate and nationwide, the overall mood was one of civic pride, and voting was remarkably smooth.

STORY ON PAGE A5

MIDSTATE VOTERS

For many, it's a time to reflect

"Look what I've seen in my lifetime," says Calobe Jackson, who has met both an ex-slave and Barack Obama. The Rev. Martin Odom says we should celebrate. "It says something about who we are as a nation."

STORY ON PAGE B1

It was the longest, the hardest-fought and the most intensely followed presidential election in a generation. In the end, Sen. Barack Obama made history with a sweeping victory to become the nation's first black president. Obama broke fundraising records thanks to millions of small donations, enlisted an army of volunteers and remade the electoral map by claiming states that Democrats had not won for decades.

COVERAGE STARTS ON PAGE A3

NATIONAL ELECTION COVERAGE ON PAGES A3-7, LOCAL ELECTION COVERAGE ON PAGES B1-4

50 cents

8 13493 00300 3

INDEX Business....A11-13 Comics....C6,7 How to reach us....A9 Obituaries....B6-8
Classified....B9-13 Crosswords....B11, C5,6 Lotteries....Page Two Public notices....B13

62° 48°
Weather, Back Page

Volume 167, No. 266
Copyright © 2008, The Patriot-News Co.

Popular vote 47,446,730 (47%) Electoral vote **141**

Totals as of 12:28 a.m. 270 electoral votes needed to win.

 Popular vote 51,313,395 (51%) Electoral vote **338** WINNER

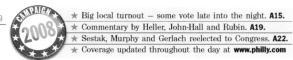

★ Big local turnout — some vote late into the night. **A15.**
★ Commentary by Heller, John-Hall and Rubin. **A19.**
★ Sestak, Murphy and Gerlach reelected to Congress. **A22.**
★ Coverage updated throughout the day at **www.philly.com**

WEDNESDAY NOV. 5, 2008

The Philadelphia Inquirer

75¢ $1 in some locations outside the metropolitan area

philly●com

City & Suburbs Edition c

180th Year, No. 158

President-elect Obama: "Change has come to America."

HISTORIC WIN

ELECTION SPECIAL: 14 PAGES OF COVERAGE

Milestone:

A change that resonates beyond U.S.

By Larry Eichel
INQUIRER SENIOR WRITER

Step back for a moment and consider what happened yesterday.

The people of the United States have elected an African American man named Barack Obama as their president.

Given the corrosive role of race in the American saga, this is a seminal event. Not just for this country, but for any country.

There does not appear to be a single instance in "the entire history of the human condition," to use the words of writer Shelby Steele, in which a major nation-state has chosen to put a member of such a historically downtrodden minority in charge.

"It says to everyone in America, 'You can be president someday,'" said historian Douglas Brinkley of Rice University. "It plays into our national mythology in a very real and profound way. ... This isn't
See **HISTORY** on A17

Congress:

Democrats broaden their majorities

By Tom Raum
ASSOCIATED PRESS

WASHINGTON — Democrats retained and expanded their control of the Senate yesterday, ousting Republican Sens. Elizabeth Dole of North Carolina and John Sununu of New Hampshire and capturing seats held by retiring GOP senators in Virginia and New Mexico.

With 29 of 35 Senate races called, Democrats were guaranteed at least a 55-45 majority, including two holdover independents who vote with Democrats. But they were hoping for even greater gains in a political environment that clearly favored them.

New Jersey Democrat John Adler narrowly defeated Republican Chris Myers in the pivotal race for the state's Third Congressional District. In other House
See **CONGRESS** on A22

PABLO MARTINEZ MONSIVAIS / Associated Press
Amid a sea of cheers and joyful tears, President-elect Obama takes the stage at an election-night celebration for hundreds of thousands of supporters in Chicago's Grant Park last night.

DAVID MAIALETTI / Staff Photographer
A jubilant crowd at Broad and Chestnut Streets celebrates President-elect Barack Obama's victory. Shortly after 11 p.m., when the television networks called the election in Obama's favor, thousands of young people began traveling down Broad Street to gather outside City Hall for an impromptu celebration. **A19.**

The vote:

Pa., Ohio and Fla. help fuel the victory.

By Thomas Fitzgerald
INQUIRER STAFF WRITER

Democrat Barack Obama, the 47-year-old son of a black father from Kenya and a white mother from Kansas, decisively won election yesterday as the nation's first African American president, a victory that seemed unthinkable a generation ago.

Embracing Obama's message of hope and call for change in the direction of the country, voters repudiated an unpopular president and his party during a time of war and economic uncertainty. In cities across the nation, crowds spilled into the streets to celebrate, including outside the White House.

The first-term senator from Illinois will be sworn in Jan. 20 as the 44th president, and Sen. Joseph R. Biden Jr. of Delaware as vice president.

Republican John McCain called Obama to concede a little after 11 p.m., bringing to a close a marathon presidential campaign of nearly two years. President Bush also called to congratulate him.

"If there is anyone out there who still doubts that America is a place where all things are possible, who still wonders if the dream of our founders is alive in our time, who still questions the power of our democracy, tonight is your answer," Obama told hundreds of thousands of delirious supporters gathered last night in Chicago's Grant Park.

"Change has come to America," he said.

Obama's convincing win, along with the Democrats' congressional majorities, could provide momentum to his policy priorities he promised in the campaign: withdrawal from Iraq; health-care insurance for all; and a
See **VOTE** on A8

INSIDE

NBC10 **WEATHER**
High 62, Low 54

Breezy today with periods of rain today and tomorrow. Air quality: Good to moderate. Full report and NBC10 EarthWatch forecast, **B11.**

INDEX
Classifieds **D1**
Comics **E8**
Editorials **A24**
Express / Lotteries **F12**
Social Circuit **E4**
Obituaries **B8**
Television **E6**

ADVERTISEMENT

Region lined up for day to remember

For this historic vote, long lines and rain kept few away.

By Alfred Lubrano
INQUIRER STAFF WRITER

As though responding to a rung bell, Philadelphia-area residents drained out of condos and cul-de-sacs, rowhouses and split-levels, to stand in rain and long lines yesterday so that they could choose the leader of the free world.

Cynics who said they had never paid attention to elections before were queuing up beside first-time voters giddy to participate, themselves standing next to faithful electors for whom picking a president was sacred duty.

"We've never seen anything like this," said ward leader Janet Chrzan in the Brookline section of Haverford Township — a notion echoed throughout the area, as record numbers of voters turned out on a day that crackled with portent and felt like history.

In an American exercise linking Allegheny Avenue to Cody, Wyo., the Main Line to the Florida Panhandle, people in this region added vote upon vote to a blossoming national aggregate.

And it changed the country overnight.

"I'm ready for a change," said
See **DAY** on A14

53

At a critical moment before the Pennsylvania primary, Obama delivered a widely hailed speech on race relations at Philadelphia's Constitution Center.

★ ★ ★ SPECIAL EDITION ★ ★ ★

Volume 124, No. 102   Wednesday, November 5, 2008   Price 75¢

 # THE PHILADELPHIA TRIBUNE
www.phillytrib.com

2008 PRESIDENTIAL ELECTION

OBAMA WINS

Senator Becomes First African-American Elected President Of The United States

❋ Takes Pennsylvania   ❋ McCain concedes defeat   ❋ Biden is VP-Elect

54

The oldest continually published black newspaper in America has served Philadelphia's African American community since 1884. Its front reflected the historic moment and, for its readership, a promise a long time coming.

Barack Obama addresses a crowd of a quarter million people in Chicago after he won the presidential election on Tuesday night. *AP PHOTO*

Eric Mayes
Tribune Staff Writer

In one of the nation's most historic elections, Barack Obama swept to victory last night, becoming the first Black man to win the presidency of the United States. Triumphant, Obama broke the race barrier in a country that has long battled its legacy of slavery, Jim Crow laws and lingering racial disparities.

"If there is anyone out there who still doubts that America is a place where all things are possible, who still wonders if the dream of our founders is alive in our time, who still questions the power of our democracy, tonight is your answer," said Obama, speaking to a roaring Chicago crowd shortly before midnight. "I will never forget who this victory truly belongs to. It belongs to you. Change has come to America."

He congratulated his opponent, Sen. John McCain, and returned to his campaign theme of unity saying it was needed to move the country forward.

"Sen. McCain fought long and hard in this campaign and he's fought even longer and harder for the country that he loves," Obama said. "He has endured sacrifices for America that most of us cannot begin to imagine. We are better off for the service rendered by this selfless leader. I congratulate him I congratulate Gov. (Sarah) Palin for all that they have achieved and I look forward to working with them to renew this nation's promise in the months ahead."

Not only did he sweep the nation. Obama also won in a landslide in Pennsylvania — a battleground state with 21 electoral votes, that supported his opponent Hillary Clinton in the June primary.

The networks called Pennsylvania for Obama before 9 p.m.

McCain conceded at about 11:20 p.m. after it became clear that California, Oregon, Washington and Virginia, too, had decided in his opponent's favor.

"The American people and they have spoken clearly," he said, speaking to a gathering of supporters gathered in Phoenix, Ariz., who booed as he spoke of his defeat. "A little while ago I had the honor of calling Sen. Obama to congratulate him on being elected the president of the country we both love. In a contest as long and difficult .as this campaign has been, his success alone commands my respect."

In Philadelphia, McCain's concession was greeted with honking car horns in the streets where shouts of "Obama" could also be heard.

"Let there be no reason now for any American to fail to cherish their citizenship in this, the greatest nation on earth," he said, acknowledging the nation's history of racism. "Sen. Obama has achieved a great thing for himself and his country."

McCain also urged his supporters to give their support to Obama.

Election - Page 2A

Election - Page 2A

❋ More Coverage

117TH YEAR. NO. 310 | SOUTH CAROLINA'S LARGEST NEWSPAPER | COPYRIGHT © 2008 | CAPITAL FINAL ++

The State

WEDNESDAY, NOVEMBER 5, 2008

History.

GETTY IMAGES

President-elect Barack Obama and his children, Sasha, 7, and Malia, 10, and his wife, Michelle, celebrate his victory at a rally in Grant Park in Chicago.

'Change has come to America,' President-elect Barack Obama said, describing this country as the place 'where all things are possible.' His rival John McCain conceded, saying he recognized the significance of the election for African-Americans and 'the special pride that must be theirs tonight.'

DEMS HOPE FOR FILIBUSTER-PROOF SENATE

Democrats ousted incumbent Republican Sens. Elizabeth Dole in North Carolina and John Sununu in New Hampshire as they pushed toward winning 60 seats in the U.S. Senate. **Page S7**

GRAHAM GLIDES TO RE-ELECTION

A well-funded U.S. Sen. Lindsey Graham swept past a little-known Democrat to win a 2nd term in Washington. **Page S6**

WILSON, CLYBURN KEEP HOUSE SEATS

U.S. House members Joe Wilson and Jim Clyburn kept opponents at bay in South Carolina's 2nd and 6th Congressional Districts. **Page S6**

South Carolina chooses McCain

Primary favorite John McCain won a solidly red South Carolina on Tuesday. Energized by the U.S. presidential race, voters waited in long lines across South Carolina — and went for McCain by a double-digit margin. **Page S4**

IN THE HOUSE, AGAIN: BLACK REPUBLICANS

Republican Tim Scott of Charleston County has made S.C. history, becoming the first black GOP member to win a House seat in about 100 years. **Page S11**

S.C. SENATE NOW ALL-MALE

South Carolina has earned a new dubious title: It's the only state with an all-male Senate. All three female candidates vying for seats, including one in Lexington County, were defeated. **Page S8**

DISTRICT 5 VOTERS SAY YES TO BOND

District 5 voters, who rebuffed earlier bond proposals, gave a thumbs-up to a multimillion-dollar package for the Irmo-Chapin system. **Page S8**

6 07770 00001 0

Although several papers used "History" as a headline, this is the only one we saw that turned it into a sentence. Notice the power of that period at the end.

DECISION 2008 ★ SPECIAL COVERAGE

168ᵀᴴ YEAR
50¢
★★★★

WEDNESDAY
NOVEMBER 5, 2008
COMMERCIALAPPEAL.COM

THE
COMMERCIAL
APPEAL

ON THE WEB

**Up to the minute
election news**

COMMERCIALAPPEAL.COM

INSIDE

**12 pages of news
and analysis**

YES HE DID

HISTORY | Democrat Barack Obama becomes first black man to be elected president

NEXT STEP | Tells thousands gathered to celebrate in Chicago that 'change has come'

56

*Obama won
Tennessee's largest
county, but as in
most other southern
states, his large
margins in urban
areas didn't outweigh
the rural votes for
McCain.*

Pablo Martinez Monsivais/Associated Press

The son of a black father from Kenya and a white mother from Kansas, Barack Obama waves to thousands who gathered to celebrate his election victory Tuesday night in Chicago.

Electoral votes

State-by-state snapshot of the presidential race: 270 needed to win

■ McCain **145**   ■ Obama **338**   ▦ Too close to call

Washington
D.C. ■

Unofficial
results as of
11:30 CST

Source: Associated Press

ALL THE LATEST INFORMATION

Get updated results of all the big political contests
at **commercialappeal.com**

At 10:01 p.m. CST Tuesday, after a number of swing states including Pennsylvania, Ohio, Virginia and Florida were declared for him, Democrat Barack Obama of Illinois became the first black man elected president of the United States.

Obama sealed his victory by defeating Republican John McCain in a number of hard-fought battleground states.

As groups across the country erupted in jubilation at the news of Obama's victory, he told a huge crowd gathered in Chicago's Grant Park that his win proved the power of democracy. "They believed this time must be different, that their voices could be that difference."

After calling Obama to concede defeat, McCain spoke to his supporters in Arizona, telling them, "The American people have spoken, and spoken clearly." | **STORY, A9**

MORE INSIDE

Obama wins Shelby; GOP takes Tenn.

Still a red state: Despite Shelby County's high turnout and strong support, Obama can't turn Tennessee blue as McCain holds strong. | **A10**

Republicans hold on

Republicans hold Tenn. and Miss. seats as Democrats gain more Senate posts nationally. | **A6**

Cohen, Blackburn win

Democrat Steve Cohen and Republican Marsha Blackburn re-elected to U.S. House. | **A7**

Abundant sun

Warmth stays with us.
High 77. Low 58.

Forecast by News Channel 3

DETAILS, C4

ELECTION NEWS: AROUND THE REGION

**Referendums
in spotlight** | B1

Ballot issues: Voters take a close look at 10 issues on the city and county ballots, including term limits, staggered terms and the sale of MLGW.

**It's all about
possibilities** | B1

Wendi C. Thomas: While the election was a national litmus test on race, it was also about what America can be, and is already becoming.

**Waiting for a new
councilman** | B1

Adding up the votes: Scanner malfunction slows counting to see which of four candidates will replace Scott McCormick on the Memphis City Council.

© Copyright 2008
The Commercial Appeal
A B C D

7 49377 10040 0

For a list of top stories from
commercialappeal.com
go to page A2

Interactive Weather

Weekdays with Jim Syoen on **commercialappeal.com**

Travel outlook • Weather headlines • 5-day local forecast • Local events

Sponsored by
ALL METAL ROOFING SYSTEMS
The Tin Man

BROWNSVILLE
The Herald

WEDNESDAY, NOVEMBER 5, 2008   BORN ON THE FOURTH OF JULY 1892   50 CENTS

    PRESIDENTIAL ◆ ELECTION '08

OBAMA!

Barack claims presidency in historic election

➤ **PAGE A7**

Democratic presidential nominee Sen. Barack Obama battled Republican candidate Sen. John McCain for the support of American voters Tuesday, creating history to become the first minority to become the nation's president-elect. **For the complete story, see PAGE A7.**

2008 LOCAL RACES

COUNTY SHERIFF		U.S. SENATOR		BROWNSVILLE INDEPENDENT SCHOOL DISTRICT
LUCIO	CISNEROS	CORNYN	NORIEGA	**Who will serve on school board?**
65%	**35%**	**55%**	**43%**	➤ **PAGE A6**

*Breakdown on Cameron County votes based on unofficial returns available at press time.
➤ **PAGE A6**

*Breakdown on Cameron County votes based on unofficial returns available at press time.
➤ **PAGE A4**

Obama top choice for city's students
➤ **PAGE C1**

➤ **CONSTABLE PRECINCT 1:** REPUBLICAN CHALLENGER LEADS RACE AGAINST DEMOCRATIC INCUMBENT CONVICTED OF FELONY, **A6**

A cut-out sign of Democratic presidential candidate Sen. Barack Obama encouraged Brownsville residents to vote Tuesday as polling places opened for the presidential election. The sign was on 12th Street across from the Dancy building.

BRAD DOHERTY/
THE BROWNSVILLE
HERALD

Cameron County drawn to polls by presidential race

Cameron County voters turned out in huge numbers to cast their ballots in U.S., state and local races.
➤ **PAGE A4**

ONLINE
FOR VIDEO AND
PHOTOGRAPHS FROM
ELECTION DAY, LOG
ON TO OUR WEB SITE
BROWNSVILLEHERALD.COM

ONLINE POLL   Do you think your vote counted this election?
www.BrownsvilleHerald.com

Abby B8	Classified C7	Editorial A10	Sports B1	High **88°**	
Amusements B8	Comics B5	Television B9	Stocks B6	Low **71°**	
Calendar A5	Community A5	Horoscope B8			

57

Serving a pocket of blue on the Mexican border in red-state Texas, this paper was one of many that played on Obama's name to mark his victory.

The Dallas Morning News

Texas' Leading Newspaper   75 cents   **Dallas, Texas, Wednesday, November 5, 2008**   dallasnews.com

ELECTIONS '08 | Special Report, 14-27A

'Change has come'

Obama wins big, shatters White House color barrier

VERNON BRYANT/Staff Photographer

Barack Obama, with wife Michelle and daughters Sasha, 7, and Malia, 10, addressed a jubilant crowd at Chicago's Grant Park on Tuesday night after rival John McCain conceded the presidential election. Mr. Obama, whose victory capped the first-term U.S. senator's meteoric rise to the top of the political world, called on Americans to embrace "a new spirit of service."

DALLAS REACTION

For black residents, pride and optimism

By SCOTT FARWELL
and JESSICA MEYERS
Staff Writers

For a generation, black parents have told their children, "You can be anything you want in this world."

After Tuesday night, they can say it with confidence.

Barack Obama, a first-term senator from Illinois known for booming soliloquies and a cool-under-fire demeanor, was elected the nation's first black president.

The historic election was greeted with prayer and shouts of jubilation around the city, especially in southern Dallas, home to more than 500,000 black residents.

"Tonight, America is living up to its potential," said Ahtatcha Hendrix, a 32-year-old self-proclaimed political junkie from southern

See **CHEERING** Page 18A

Senator makes history; Dems expand majorities

By TODD J. GILLMAN
and GROMER JEFFERS JR.
Staff Writers

CHICAGO — Democrat Barack Obama smashed through the presidential color barrier Tuesday with a huge win propelled by economic malaise, war fatigue and an urgent demand for change.

"It's been a long time coming, but tonight, because of what we did on this day, in this election, at this defining moment, change has come to America," Mr. Obama told a jubilant crowd estimated at 240,000 in Grant Park after defeating Republican John McCain.

His stunning political rise — from Illinois state senator to president-elect in four years — marks an extraordinary moment for America, sending to the dustbin of history the Jim Crow legacy that persisted even when he was born

See **OBAMA** Page 19A

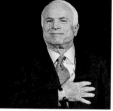

ANDREW HARRER/Bloomberg News

Mr. McCain, outside Phoenix's Biltmore Hotel, called on supporters to offer Mr. Obama "our good will and earnest effort to find ways to come together."

ANALYSIS

Walk the walk? He needs running start

By WAYNE SLATER
Senior Political Writer
wslater@dallasnews.com

AUSTIN — As mandates go, Barack Obama has been given the keys and a clear highway to steer the nation in a dramatically new direction.

From his first day in the White House, the new president will find himself as the country's crisis manager — facing the fierce urgency of huge expectations.

"He'll have to go and make things happen," said University of Texas professor Bruce Buchanan.

"He has a credible claim on tax cuts for the middle class and tax increases for the rich, for getting out of Iraq sooner rather than later and dealing in a new way with adversaries in the world," he said. "You still have to go out

See **NEW** Page 18A

Congress

House

+12

Dems get first back-to-back surge for the party since before World War II.

Senate

+5

Dems fattened majority control and were hoping for even greater gains.

President

Electoral votes by state,
270 needed to win   80% precincts reporting

Obama

338   **52%**
54,314,223
27 states
(including D.C.)

McCain

141   **47%**
49,740,554
18 states

58 electoral votes, 6 states undeclared

INSIDE

How Obama won. **15A**

Democrats build on majority in Congress. **20A**

Americans stormed to the polls in what could be record numbers, but problems were scattered and few. **22A**

 CHAT LIVE WITH Wayne Slater about the presidential election and other results at 11 a.m. today. **dallasnews.com**

SEE OUR MAPS of Dallas County precinct results for the presidency, sheriff's race, and Parkland hospital bond. **dallasnews.com/precinctresults**

Forecast: Showers
Metro, back page
©2008, The Dallas Morning News

INSIDE			
Lottery	2A	Sports TV/Radio	2C
Texas	3A	NFL	6C
Nation	4-6A	Market Day	6-7D
World	8-13,29A	TV	9E
Editorials	30A	Movies	2E
Reg. Roundup	2B	Dear Abby	9E
Obituaries	4-6B	Comics	9-11E
NBA	1C	Horoscope	13E

U.S. SENATE

Cornyn wins re-election

Republican John Cornyn fended off Democrat Rick Noriega to win re-election to the U.S. Senate. **21A**

DALLAS COUNTY

New hospital approved

In Dallas County, voters overwhelmingly approved replacing aging Parkland Memorial Hospital with a larger, modern facility.
Sheriff race: Voters chose incumbent Democrat Lupe Valdez over Lowell Cannaday. **22A**

TEXAS SENATE

Tarrant County adds more blue

In Tarrant County, Democrat Wendy Davis defeated Republican state Sen. Kim Brimer. **27A**

★ **4-PAGE PRESIDENTIAL WRAP** ★

The Salt Lake Tribune

UTAH'S INDEPENDENT VOICE SINCE 1871

OBAMA

"The road ahead will be long. Our climb will be steep.... But, America, I have never been more hopeful than I am tonight that we will get there."

VOTERS MADE HISTORY TUESDAY: They elected the first black president of the United States. Barack Obama's victory was greeted with jubilation and tears by tens of thousands who gathered in Chicago's Grant Park and millions throughout the nation. As 44th president, Obama will become the leader of a recession-stricken nation that also is at war in Iraq and Afghanistan. Tuesday night, Obama acknowledged the hard road ahead, a road that must be met with "unyielding hope" and by a nation willing to roll up its sleeves and engender a "new spirit" of sacrifice and patriotism. And he spoke directly to those who didn't vote for him: "I will be your president, too." In conceding, Sen. John McCain said Obama "has achieved a great thing for himself and his country" and vowed he would support America's new president in facing the challenges. **Details, Page 2**

TRENT NELSON/*The Salt Lake Tribune*

Shanita Star Harvell of Salt Lake City, who identifies herself as an independent, reacts Tuesday at the Radisson Hotel as Barack Obama is named the next president of the United States. "I feel that myself and this universe is one. He united the country. This is how I feel, that everything is on the right path again. A guy named Barack Obama was named president," she said.

Utahns react

For many black Utahns, the day in which a black man is elected president is far from a world they once knew. Some say the challenges that they have faced helped make this day happen. **Page 2**

Historic day

Barack Obama's election as the U.S.'s first black president is a sign of the changing times in America. **Page 3**

Barack Obama
52%

John McCain
47%

TIMOTHY A. CLARY/AFP/Getty Images

Top, President-Elect Barack Obama and his family at an election night victory rally.

59

The front page reflected Obama's national win, though McCain won Utah by twenty-nine percentage points.

60

The paper, in noting that Obama rolled to victory "even in Virginia," underscored the fact that a Democratic presidential hopeful had not won the state in the past ten tries.

Our 143rd year | 11.05.08 | PILOTONLINE.COM | 50¢

The Virginian-Pilot

Obama
AMERICA'S 44th PRESIDENT

2008

BARACK OBAMA

338

Electoral College votes.
51.3 percent of the popular vote. *

JOHN McCAIN

168

Electoral College votes.
47.5 percent of the popular vote. *

* According to tallies at press time.

ON A PROMISE OF CHANGE, SENATOR MAKES HISTORY

HE STARTED HIS CAMPAIGN invoking the spirit of Abraham Lincoln, who fought to hold the nation together after slavery ripped it apart.

The son of a Kansan and a Kenyan, he ignited the passion of millions with his promise of change.

He ended in victory, even in Virginia, at a time of war and economic turmoil. He will become the nation's first African American president. Whatever history Barack Obama goes on to make in the Oval Office, that distinction will remain.

STORY, PAGE 3

16 pages of election coverage inside. | Go to PilotOnline.com for a database of results, videos and slide shows, or to post comments.

EMMANUEL DUNAND | AFP | GETTY IMAGES FILE PHOTO

Virginia Beach

SESSOMS LEADING OBERNDORF

Will Sessoms appears poised to end Meyera Oberndorf's two decades in power. Get all local election results in **HAMPTON ROADS**

DAVID B. HOLLINGSWORTH | THE VIRGINIAN-PILOT

United States Senate

MARK WARNER
defeats
JIM GILMORE
The battle of the ex-governors goes to the Democrat, who vows "results, not rhetoric." **PAGE 7**

United States House

GLENN NYE
defeats
THELMA DRAKE
The Democratic political newcomer pulls off an upset in the 2nd District. **PAGE 6**

North Carolina

KAY HAGAN *defeats* ELIZABETH DOLE
The Democratic state senator unseats the one-term senator in a bitter campaign. **PAGE 8**

northwest ■ asianweekly

PRSRT STD
U.S. Postage Paid
Permit No. 746
Seattle, WA

Election Coverage
pages 7-11

VOL 27   NO 46 NOVEMBER 8 – NOVEMBER 14, 2008   **FREE** 26 YEARS **YOUR VOICE**

61

Obama's multiethnic coalition included Asians, 62 percent of whom voted for him. More Asian Americans have voted for Democratic presidential candidates in every election since 1992, when 31 percent voted for Bill Clinton.

412 Maynard Ave. S., Seattle, WA 98104 • t. 206.223.5559 • f. 206.223.0626 • info@nwasianweekly.com • www.nwasianweekly.com

WEDNESDAY, NOVEMBER 5, 2008

The Seattle Times

MOSTLY CLOUDY
High, 53. Low, 46.
> LOCAL B10

75¢

Independent and locally owned since 1896 | seattletimes.com
1.5 million readers weekly in Western Washington, in print and online

'CHANGE HAS COME TO AMERICA'

BARACK OBAMA, THE NATION'S 44TH PRESIDENT

GOVERNOR: Blue tide lifts Gregoire > A1, A3   **LIGHT RAIL:** Sound Transit plan passing > A6

62

Washington's mail-in balloting system, combined with the highest turnout since World War II, meant that although the state was called for Obama on election night, all of the votes weren't counted for a couple of weeks.

TIMOTHY A. CLARY / AFP/GETTY IMAGES

Barack Obama and his family arrive on stage for a victory rally at Grant Park in Chicago after Americans on Tuesday elected the senator as their first black president.

VICTORY BREAKS RACIAL BARRIER

McCain concedes just after polls close in West

BY MICHAEL D. SHEAR
AND ROBERT BARNES
The Washington Post

WASHINGTON – Barack Obama was elected the nation's 44th president Tuesday, riding a reformist message of change and an inspirational exhortation of hope to become the first African American to ascend to the White House.

Obama, 47, the son of a Kenyan father and a white mother from Kansas, led a tide of Democratic victories across the nation in defeating Republican John McCain, a 26-year veteran of Washington who could not overcome his connections to President Bush's increasingly unpopular administration.

"If there is anyone out there who still doubts that America is a place where all things are possible, who still wonders if the dream of our founders is alive in our time, who still questions the power of our democracy, tonight is your answer," Obama told tens of thousands of supporters during a victory celebration in Chicago's Grant Park.

"It's been a long time coming, but tonight, because of what we did on this day, in this election, at this defining moment, change has come to America."

Obama became the first Democrat since Jimmy Carter in 1976 to receive more than 50 percent of the
Please see > OBAMA, A10

THOMAS JAMES HURST / THE SEATTLE TIMES

IN DOWNTOWN SEATTLE, *hundreds of people flood into the streets, chanting "Yes, we can" as they celebrate Obama's victory Tuesday night.*

Election '08

10 pages inside

LOCAL

ASSISTED SUICIDE: Voters approve I-1000, modeled after Oregon law. > A3

8TH DISTRICT: Rep. Dave Reichert and Darcy Burner locked in a tight rematch. > A5

CHEERS FOR OBAMA: Local churchgoers rejoice. > A11

NATIONAL

U.S. SENATE: Democrats widen lead; Dole unseated. > A8

U.S. HOUSE: Last Republican in New England is ousted. > A8

○ WEB EXTRA
Latest election results
Go to seattletimes.com

Electoral vote count

349 OBAMA   MCCAIN 163

270 electoral votes needed

Gregoire appears headed to victory; Burner, Reichert in close race

BY JIM BRUNNER
Seattle Times staff reporter

Gov. Christine Gregoire appeared headed toward a second term last night, lifted by the blue tide that swept fellow Democrat Barack Obama to the presidency.

Obama racked up a huge victory in the state, sending thousands of people to celebrate in the streets of Seattle.

Meanwhile, Gregoire had a substantial lead over Republican Dino Rossi in their bitter rematch. While only about half the votes were counted Tuesday night, the trend favored Gregoire since the vast majority of remaining ballots were in King, Snohomish and Pierce counties, where she was running strong.

But Rossi contended not enough votes had been counted to declare a victor.

Democrats were eyeing another possible pickup here, as Democratic challenger Darcy Burner was running neck and neck with Republican Congressman
Please see > STATE, A2

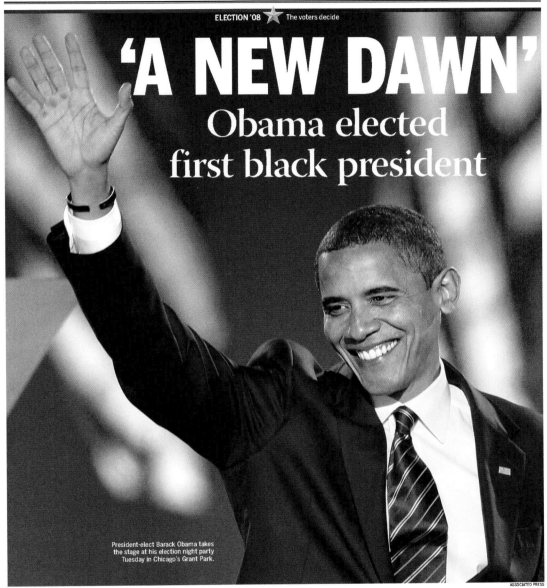

JSOnline.com

WEDNESDAY: NOVEMBER 5, 2008   C   FINAL: METRO

MILWAUKEE • WISCONSIN

JOURNAL SENTINEL

2008 PULITZER PRIZE WINNER FOR LOCAL REPORTING

ELECTION '08   The voters decide

'A NEW DAWN'

Obama elected first black president

President-elect Barack Obama takes the stage at his election night party Tuesday in Chicago's Grant Park.

ASSOCIATED PRESS

63

This paper's staff–written story notes the "epic and exhaustive campaign that consumed Americans and captivated much of the world."

ELECTION RESULTS

COVERAGE ON PAGES 3A-11A, 1B, 6B-8B; UPDATES AT JSONLINE.COM

U.S. CONGRESS

Kagen beats Gard

U.S. Rep Steve Kagen (D-Wis.) scores a narrow victory over challenger John Gard in the 8th Congressional District race. **1B**

JOE KOSHOLLEK/JOURNAL SENTINEL
Steve Kagen addresses supporters after defeating John Gard.

Democrats gain in House, Senate

With 29 of 35 Senate races called, Democrats are guaranteed at least a 56-44 majority, but they hope for even greater gains. In the House, Democrats are expected to gain upwards of 20 seats. **5A**

MILWAUKEE

Paid sick leave issue approved

City of Milwaukee residents overwhelmingly approve requiring private employers to provide paid sick leave for all their workers. **7B**

Sales tax may pass: A referendum on raising Milwaukee County's sales tax by 1 percentage point appears headed for approval. **6B**

WISCONSIN

Democrats hold state Senate, gain in Assembly

Democrats appear to keep control of the state Senate, but their margin depends on the outcomes of elections that are too close to call. Democrats make gains in the state Assembly, putting them in striking distance of taking control of the house for the first time in 14 years. **1B, 7B**

Candidate's call for change resonates around nation

By CRAIG GILBERT
cgilbert@journalsentinel.com

Illinois Sen. Barack Obama made history Tuesday, becoming the first African-American to win the presidency of the United States after an epic and exhaustive campaign that consumed Americans and captivated much of the world.

PRESIDENT
U.S. results
151,906 of 187,088 units reporting
Barack Obama (D)...55,015,187
John McCain (R)....50,337,843
Wisconsin results
3,119 of 3,621 units reporting
Barack Obama (D) ...1,380,528
John McCain (R).......1,047,037
For latest results go to www.jsonline.com

Hungry for change, steeped in discontent and economically embattled, voters turned to a candidate whose election would have been hard to envision in decades past, who was a political unknown five years ago, who defeated two entrenched political figures on his way to the White House in John McCain and Hillary Rodham Clinton, and who rewrote the campaign book getting there.

"It's been a long time coming, but tonight, because of what we did on this day, in this election, at this defining moment, change has come to America," Obama told a huge crowd of supporters in Chicago, saying a "new dawn of American leadership is at hand."

Addressing the world beyond America's shores, Oba-

Please see **OBAMA, 9A**

IT'S THE ECONOMY, POLLS SAY
Economy was on the majority of voters' minds. **6A**

▶ **More of Wisconsin votes blue in '08:** Youth, independents choose Obama. **11A**

▶ **Living to see the day:** Black Milwaukeeans celebrate. **4A**

▶ **Party in Kenya:** Obama's relatives celebrate. **4A**

A WORD   **Elation** (ee LAY shuhn) A feeling of exultant joy or pride. n. **Page 9G**

INDEX   Comics 7G   Movies 9G
Crossword 8G   Stocks 4D
Deaths 4B   Sports on TV 7C
Editorials 18A   TV listings 9G

WEATHER
TODAY'S TMJ4   Map: Back of Sports

TODAY
53/71
Partly cloudy and unseasonably warm

TOMORROW
54/63
Mostly cloudy, showers and storms

7   31544 10500   4

50¢
CITY AND SUBURBS
$1.00 OR HIGHER
ELSEWHERE

DREAM FULFILLED A11

Analysis: Now Obama has to get down to business A11

Wyoming Tribune Eagle

WEDNESDAY, NOVEMBER 5, 2008 · CHEYENNE, WYOMING · WYOMINGNEWS.COM · 75¢

Herbert: 4% / Trauner: 42% / Lummis: 53%

NEW U.S. REP: LUMMIS

Republican candidate for U.S. House of Representatives Cynthia Lummis celebrates after receiving a phone call informing her that she won her election bid over Gary Trauner Tuesday night at the Nagle-Warren Mansion. Michael Smith/staff **See story on page A13**

Mockler: 42% / Kaysen: 57%

NEW MAYOR: KAYSEN

From left, Dorothe Akes, Billie Miller, Rick Kaysen and Jim Murphy watch election returns on Tuesday night at the Plains Hotel just before Kaysen was elected to be the next mayor of the city of Cheyenne. Larry Brinlee/staff

By Jodi Rogstad
jrogstad@wyomingnews.com

CHEYENNE – Rick Kaysen easily coasted to victory to become the Capital City's next mayor, posting a strong lead from the early results until the last absentee ballot was counted.

Kaysen, 62, garnered 14,565 votes to state Sen. Jayne Mockler's 10,711.

"Needless to say, I'm very pleased, overwhelmed at the same time and relieved now that the citizens have had their voices heard," Kaysen said. "(I feel) pretty doggone good."

The former CEO of Cheyenne Light, Fuel and Power ran on a platform of reforming downtown, bringing better jobs to Cheyenne and keeping the progressive bent of Mayor Jack Spiker's administration.

"I think we're going to have a very strong council," Kaysen said.

All the incumbents won re-election, except Ward 1 Councilman Pete Laybourn.

"I think we can bring some strengths and talents to move the community forward."

See Kaysen, page A2

ELECTION 2008 ELECTION WINNERS

Full list of voting results Page A7
Stories on every winner Pages A6-A14

MIKE ENZI (R)
U.S. SENATOR

JOHN BARRASSO (R)
U.S. SENATOR

WAYNE JOHNSON (R)
SENATE DIST. 6

BRYAN PEDERSEN (R)
HOUSE DIST. 7

LORI MILLIN (D)
HOUSE DIST. 8

DAVE ZWONITZER (R)
HOUSE DIST. 9

PETE ANDERSON (R)
HOUSE DIST. 10

AMY EDMONDS (R)
HOUSE DIST. 12

KEN ESQUIBEL (D)
HOUSE DIST. 41

DAN ZWONITZER (R)
HOUSE DIST. 43

JAMES BYRD (D)
HOUSE DIST. 44

AMBER ASH
COUNCIL WARD 1

JIMMY VALDEZ
COUNCIL WARD 1

JACK SPIKER
COUNCIL WARD 2

PAT COLLINS
COUNCIL WARD 2

JIM BROWN
COUNCIL WARD 3

DON PIERSON
COUNCIL WARD 3

LCSD1 trustees (4-year)
Jan Stalcup
Bob Farwell
Glenn Garcia

LCSD1 trustees (2-year)
Hank Bailey

LCSD2 trustees (2-year)
Jeff Kirkbride

LCSD2 trustees (4-year)
Esther Davison (Area C)
Sue Anderson (Area D)
Julianne Randall (Area E)
Wyoema Thompson (Area E)
Jack Bomhoff (Area F)

LCCC trustees
William "Bill" Dubois
John Kaiser
Tony Mendoza
Greg Thomas

Weather
Record: 70/4
Average: 50/26
40 26
Scattered snow showers are possible today as cold air settles over southeast Wyoming

Colorado Lottery
Cash 5: 4, 16, 22, 23, 31

Index
Astrograph B9
Comics B8
Crossword B8
Dear Abby B9
Entertainment B7
Money C1
Obituaries ... A4-A5
Sudoku/Jumble ... B9

6 85504 00300 1

FINAL SCORES

Your guide to the election

Results '08

528 races across USA

■ Also, interactive map at politics.usatoday.com has latest on 3,100 counties

Wednesday, November 5, 2008

USA TODAY

NO. 1 IN THE USA

Congressional races

By Ellen Ozier, Reuters

Kay Hagan: Defeats Elizabeth Dole.

Democrats tighten grip on Senate

■ Dole ousted in North Carolina; Warner wins in Virginia, 11-13A

America makes history
Obama wins

ELECTION 2008

'Change has come to America,' he says after election to presidency erases a racial barrier; Democrats make gains

Where the race was won

Florida
McCain 49%
✓Obama 51%
99% of the vote

Colorado
McCain 45%
✓Obama 53%
69% of the vote

Ohio
McCain 47%
✓Obama 51%
85% of the vote

Pennsylvania
McCain 44%
✓Obama 55%
99% of the vote

Virginia
McCain 48%
✓Obama 52%
98% of the vote

How the states voted
As of 2:10 a.m. ET today

■ McCain　■ Obama　Undecided

More detailed map. 15A

Source: The Associated Press　By Julie Snider, USA TODAY

Newsline

■ News　■ Money　■ Sports　■ Life

Chicago celebrates Obama victory

'Is this real?' reveler asks; others pray, weep. 3A.
► Michelle Obama's focus on family. 3A.

Gay-marriage ban gains in California

Constitutional amendments also lead in Arizona, Florida; two states loosen marijuana laws. 18A.
► Democrats win statehouse in Missouri. 13A.

■ **Money: Winner faces economic mess**

President-elect will need plan of action to deal with urgent marketplace issues. 1B.
► Stocks post bigger gains under Democrats. 1B.

©COPYRIGHT 2008　USA TODAY, a division of Gannett Co., Inc.
Subscriptions, customer service
1-800-USA-0001
www.usatodayservice.com

The new first family: Barack Obama and his wife, Michelle, and daughters, Sasha, 7, and Malia, 10, greet supporters in Chicago on Tuesday.

By Jack Gruber, USA TODAY

Taps into the public's anger over economy and war

By William M. Welch
USA TODAY

Democrat Barack Obama secured a historic presidential victory Tuesday, shattering a racial barrier that once seemed unbreakable by tapping voter anger over the sinking economy and a long-running war.

Obama swept at least seven states that President Bush carried in 2004, including Florida, Virginia and Ohio, as he reshaped the political map. Republican John McCain saw his candidacy crushed under the weight of an unpopular GOP president and his own vigorous support for the Iraq war.

Obama, 47, will be the first African-American president and one of the youngest. Just four years ago, the son of a Kenyan father and a white woman from Kansas was elected to the Senate from Illinois.

"It's been a long time coming," Obama told more than 200,000 supporters jammed around Chicago's Grant Park. "Because of what we did on this day, in this election, in this defining moment, change has come to America."

The crowd chanted "Yes, we can" as emotions flowed. Obama recalled the grandmother who raised him and died two days before the triumph that will make him the nation's 44th president.

"I'm almost past words," said Clara Jones, 58, a retired store manager in Chicago. "This is something I hoped I'd see but never expected to see in my lifetime . . . We can't stop smiling."

McCain congratulated Obama and conceded before a tearful crowd of supporters in Phoenix. "The American people have spoken, and they have spoken clearly," the Arizona senator said.

"This is a historic election, and I recognize the special significance it has for African Americans and for the special pride that must be theirs tonight."

That a person of Obama's background won the White House is remarkable in a nation where race relations are still sometimes tense. Only four decades ago, when Obama was 4 years old, Congress passed the Voting Rights Act to ensure blacks can vote.

He won at least 338 electoral votes, far more than the 270 necessary, and became the first Democrat since 1976 to capture a popular-vote majority.

Obama swept Democrats to victory across the country: His party gained at least five Senate seats in Colorado, Virginia, North Carolina, New Hampshire and New Mexico and picked up at least 11 House seats. Among the ousted GOP senators was North Carolina's Elizabeth Dole, a White House hopeful in 2000. Democrat Jay Nixon was elected Missouri's governor.

For McCain, 72, a former Navy pilot and prisoner of war in Vietnam, the loss likely ended his White House dreams. He fell short of the GOP nomination in 2000 and was among the oldest nominees ever.

Surveys of voters as they left polling places showed broad support for Obama, especially among young voters, women and minorities.

Strong voter interest was visible in lines at polls in many states — evidence of a likely record turnout. A much-feared meltdown at the polls failed to materialize. Scattered problems included hours-long delays caused by faulty malfunctioning machines.

Contributing: Martha T. Moore in Chicago

In Congress, a Democratic wave

Economic concerns fuel a 'turning point' in politics

By Susan Page
USA TODAY

WASHINGTON — America's election of an African American as president wasn't the only breakthrough Tuesday night.

By defeating John McCain in such reliably Republican states as Colorado and Virginia – capital of the Confederacy and a state that hasn't backed a Democrat for president in four decades – Barack Obama reshaped the electoral map that has defined American politics for a generation.

Surveys of voters as they left polling places na-

Cover story

tionwide also showed shifts in allegiances among young people, Hispanics, upscale voters and others that could reverberate through future elections.

Obama's victory and Democratic gains in the House and Senate led Democrats to their strongest governing position since the post-Watergate election in 1976. Among the Republicans who lost re-election bids were North Carolina Sen. Elizabeth Dole and New Hampshire Sen. John Sununu, members of two of the GOP's signature families.

Some analysts see a turning point in American politics like what occurred in 1980, when Republican Ronald Reagan's victory over President Carter set the nation on a more conserva-

Please see COVER STORY next page ►

By H. Darr Beiser, USA TODAY

John McCain: At outdoor rally in Phoenix.

McCain: 'People have spoken'

■ Republican candidate concedes and pledges his support to Obama, 7A

65

The paper sold out of its 2.8 million copies of the November 5 edition, which was 380,000 more than normal, and then printed another 52,000 copies.

THE WALL STREET JOURNAL.

DOWJONES · A News Corporation Company · ★ ★ ★ ★ ★ · WEDNESDAY, NOVEMBER 5, 2008 · VOL. CCLII NO. 108 · ★ ★ ★ ★ $2.00

DJIA 9625.28 ▲ 305.45 3.3% | NASDAQ 1780.12 ▲ 3.1% | NIKKEI 9114.60 ▲ 6.3% | DJ STOXX 50 2436.01 ▲ 4.1% | 10-YR TREAS ▲ 1 5/32, yield 3.765% | OIL $70.53 ▲ $6.62 | GOLD $756.00 ▲ $30.60 | EURO $1.3001 | YEN 99.78

Obama Sweeps to Historic Victory

Nation Elects Its First African-American President Amid Record Turnout; Turmoil in Economy Dominates Voters' Concerns

BY JONATHAN WEISMAN
AND LAURA MECKLER

WASHINGTON—Sen. Barack Obama was elected the nation's first African-American president, defeating Sen. John McCain decisively Tuesday as citizens surged to the polls in a presidential race that climaxed amid the worst financial crisis since the Great Depression.

The culmination of the epic two-year campaign marks a historic moment in a nation that since its founding has struggled with racial divisions. It also ushers in a period of dominance for Democrats in Washington for the first time since the early years of President Bill Clinton's first term. With Tuesday's elections, Sen. Obama's party will control both houses of Congress as well as the White House, setting the scene for Democrats to push an ambitious agenda from health care to financial regulation to ending the war in Iraq.

In becoming the U.S.'s 44th president, Illinois Sen. Obama, 47 years old, defeated Arizona Sen. McCain, 72, a veteran lawmaker and Vietnam War hero. Despite a reputation for bucking his own party, Sen. McCain could not overcome a Democratic tide, which spurred voters to take a risk on a candidate with less than four years of national political experience. Sen. Obama is the first northern Democrat elected president since John F. Kennedy in 1960.

Also elected: Joe Biden of Delaware as vice president, the veteran senator who has promised to help Sen. Obama steer his agenda through Congress.

Sen. Obama's victory was built on record fund raising and a vast national campaign network. It remade the electoral map that had held fast for eight years. He overwhelmed reliable Democratic strongholds in the Northeast and West Coast. He won big in the industrial Midwest and contested fiercely in areas of traditional Republican strength. He won Virginia, the first time a Democratic candidate had taken the state since Lyndon Johnson in 1964. And he finally wrested Florida and Ohio from the GOP, two states that had bedeviled his party in the last two elections.

The president-elect will enter office with a long policy wish list that includes ending the war in Iraq, implementing a near-universal health-insurance plan and finding alternatives to Middle Eastern oil. All this will have to be carried out amid record budget deficits, a looming crisis in Social Security and Medicare spending as the baby-boom generation retires and fears that the nation is on the edge of a deep recession.

Democrats have touted the prospect of a big sweep not just as a partisan conquest but as an ideological turning point, one that could reverse the last great shift in 1980, when Ronald Reagan ushered in a period dominated by tax-cutting conservatism and muscular foreign policy.

It's a startling turnaround from just four years ago, when Republicans controlled Congress and the White House, and benefited from a conservative majority on the Supreme Court. The
Please turn to page A6

WINNING SMILE: Sen. Barack Obama became the nation's first African-American president, riding a historic turnout amid voter discontent with the economy to defeat Sen. John McCain.

Obama
338
electoral votes
51% of popular vote

McCain
140
electoral votes
48% of popular vote

(270 electoral votes needed to win)
As of 12:15 a.m. EST. Please visit WSJ.com for complete results
Source: Associated Press projections

Democrats Expand Majorities In Congress

BY GREG HITT
AND BRODY MULLINS

WASHINGTON—Democrats strengthened their majorities in both houses of Congress and moved close to a level of domination in the Senate that could enable them to push through major legislation.

Combined with Sen. Barack Obama's victory in the presidential race, the congressional results gave Democrats broad power in Washington that they haven't enjoyed in decades.

The Democratic gains represented the final repudiation of the Republican revolution of 1994, marking the second straight strong showing for Democrats in congressional elections. The results return the balance of power that prevailed on Capitol Hill for much of the 20th century, when Democratic-controlled Congresses were the launching pad for Social Security, the modern social safety net and civil-rights legislation.

Democratic leaders have an agenda that harks back to that era, with plans to give government a bigger role in guiding the economy and to strengthen the ability of labor unions to organize in the workplace. They also aim to expand health-insurance coverage and push through a sweeping bill to curb greenhouse-gas emissions.

"This is a tectonic-plate election, one of those once-in-a-generation times where people not only define change, but define a new relationship with government," said New York Sen.
Please turn to page A10

What's News—

Business & Finance

The Dow Jones Industrial Average soared 305.45 points, or 3.3%, ahead of election results. The close at 9625.28 was the highest in nearly a month. Oil prices rose, back above $70 a barrel. Rallies continued early Wednesday in Asia, with the Nikkei up 3.2% in midday trading after Tuesday's 6.3% gain. **C1, C5, C9**

■ **The benchmark** yield curve in major government bond markets has steepened significantly, signaling a long road to economic recovery. **C2**

■ **Businesses** are bracing for tighter financial regulation and sweeping health-care changes as Democratic power in Washington grows. **A4**

■ **Boeing said** it needs to replace thousands of improperly installed fasteners on the first Dreamliner jets before they can be flown. **B1**

■ **Online retailers** expect holiday sales growth to slow, but many forecast ringing up at least a 15% sales gain. **B2**

■ **Dell laid out** plans to cut spending, including a hiring freeze and a reduction in contract workers. **B5**

■ **Several big companies** fear the launch of new top-level domains will raise the cost of protecting their brands. **B4**

■ **The FCC is investigating** why some cable-TV subscribers are paying the same fees even as they lose channels. **B3**

■ **Archer Daniels** will produce ethanol from sugar cane in Brazil through a joint venture with Grupo Cabrera. **B1**

■ **Managed futures funds** that follow trends have soared on the dollar's rally and the collapse in commodities. **C1**

■ **D.R. Horton** expects a net loss of $800 million to $900 million in its fiscal fourth quarter. **B7**

■ **Marks & Spencer's profit** fell 43% on flat sales as shoppers defected to less-expensive rivals. **B4**

■ **Drug makers** are targeting emerging markets such as Brazil, Russia, India and China as sales slow in the U.S. **B1**

World-Wide

■ **Obama was elected the first African-American president.** The Illinois senator decisively defeated McCain as citizens thronged to the polls amid the worst financial crisis since the Depression. Obama's victory was built on record fund raising and a vast campaign network. He captured reliable Democratic strongholds in the Northeast and West Coast, won big in the industrial Midwest, prevailed in Virginia and wrested Florida and Ohio from the Republican Party. **A1-A14**
The transition to an Obama administration could begin almost immediately, with a Treasury team to soon be in place.

■ **Democrats bolstered** their majorities in Congress and were moving close to a level of Senate domination that could pave the way for major legislation. **A1**

■ **Democrats were expected** to maintain their majority in state capitols and possibly win an additional governorship. **A4**

■ **A Congo rebel leader** vowed insurgents would march on the capital after the government rejected his demand for talks. **A18**

■ **Pakistan's president** headed to Saudi Arabia to plead for aid. Zardari also pressed Petraeus to stop U.S. missile strikes.

■ **Iran's parliament** impeached and dismissed the interior minister, an Ahmadinejad ally, for faking his university degrees. **A19**

■ **Bombs exploded** at a market and bus station in Baghdad, killing 15 people, as violence increased after a week of calm.

■ **Colombia's army chief** resigned over the military's alleged killings of civilians to inflate guerrilla body counts. **A19**

■ **House lawmakers** are pressuring the Pentagon to release congressionally approved funds for an Air Force fighter. **A17**

■ **China and Taiwan agreed** to expand flights between them and allow direct shipping links for the first time. **A20**

■ **Two top Mexican officials,** including the powerful interior minister, died when their small plane crashed. **A18**

■ **Israel launched** an airstrike on Gaza after its troops clashed with Hamas militants. **A20**

Follow the news all day at WSJ.com

The New Landscape

■ Gerald Seib on challenges for Democrats A6
■ A battle for the soul of the Republican Party A3
■ A momentous day for African-Americans A8

■ See WSJ.com for full state-by-state election results.

As Economic Crisis Peaked, Tide Turned Against McCain

BY MONICA LANGLEY

The presidential race entered a critical three-day period in September when the economic crisis cast the candidates' differences in sharp relief.

On Sept. 24, with financial markets verging on panic and the economy thudding, Democratic Sen. Barack Obama placed a call to rival John McCain. He wanted to suggest they issue a joint statement on proposed financial-bailout legislation. As hours went by without a return call, Obama aides emailed each other, asking, "Have you heard anything?" One answered: "The McCain camp is cooking up something."

Later that day, Sen. McCain went before the cameras to say he was suspending his campaign to focus on helping craft the legislation. "What does that mean—suspend the campaign?" Sen.

Obama asked his staff on the trail, according to aides. At a news conference in Florida, he said, "it's going to be part of the president's job to be able to deal with more than one thing at once."

Beyond the economic tumult, troubles in the McCain camp had contributed to the Republican's extraordinary move. These included a shaky performance by his running mate in a mock debate and an admonition to Sen. McCain by some major donors to quit blasting Wall Street and focus on solutions. Suspending the campaign, one McCain adviser recalls hoping, would let them "push the reset button."

The next day, while conservative House Republicans maneuvered behind the scenes to block the bailout bill, Sen. McCain sat largely silent at a crisis summit at the White House. Afterward, Sen. Obama called his staff from

his car: "I've never seen anything like this," he said, according to several aides. "Some of the Republicans are clueless. Bush and I were trying to convince them."

The presidential candidates were essentially tied at the time, a Wall Street Journal/NBC News poll showed, with Sen. McCain just a point behind. But in the next few weeks, as the handling of the economic crisis overshadowed all other issues, Sen. Obama opened a 10-point lead. Although Sen. McCain began to gain some ground at the end, he never fully recovered from the pivotal late-September juncture.

Sen. Obama's recipe for victory, of course, had many ingredients: a record $640 million haul of donations, a vast network of campaign workers, his stance against the Iraq war, his success in portraying his foe as heir to an
Please turn to the next page

Campaign Addicts Now Confront The Morning After

* * *

As Election Coverage Fades, News Junkies Break Old Habits; Getting to Know the Kids

BY KEVIN HELLIKER
AND DAVID KESMODEL

At age 53, Anne Summers discovered a susceptibility she never knew she had. She was an election junkie.

Her affliction started with late-night news programs, then progressed to incessant Internet surfing. It culminated in door-to-door campaigning for Sen. Barack Obama near her home in Fairfax County, Va. "Addiction wouldn't be too strong a word," she says.

So today, Dr. Summers will experience a sense of emptiness familiar to recovering addicts. Never mind that she is a soccer mom, wife and full-time cardiologist. The election is over.

"To fill the void I've bought some poli-sci books," says Dr. Summers. "And I'll catch up on my medical journals."

The end of the most-followed

presidential campaign in recent years will leave many Americans feeling lost, even if their candidate won. The 2008 race provided drama and suspense to a nation hooked on reality television, mystery novels and Hollywood epics.

Arin N. Reeves, a Chicago-based diversity consultant, says she lost hours of sleep to late-night cravings for new campaign developments. For her, the vice-presidential picks were among the many suspenseful episodes—with the emergence of Gov. Sarah Palin deliciously surprising. "Week after week after week the story just kept getting better," she says.

Seldom in American history has a presidential campaign offered such compelling narratives: The rise and fall of former first lady Sen. Hillary Clinton. The come-from-behind primary
Please turn to page A8

© Copyright 2008 Dow Jones & Company. All Rights Reserved

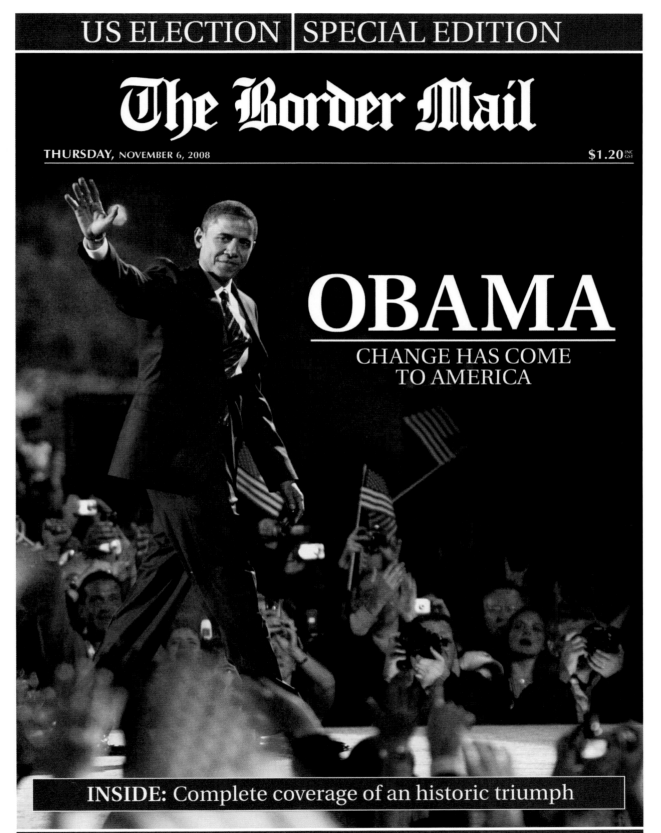

US ELECTION | SPECIAL EDITION

The Border Mail

THURSDAY, NOVEMBER 6, 2008

$1.20 INC GST

OBAMA
CHANGE HAS COME TO AMERICA

INSIDE: Complete coverage of an historic triumph

67

This 25,000–circulation Australian daily published a special section reflecting the impact of the U.S. election around the globe.

UNABHÄNGIGE TAGESZEITUNG FÜR ÖSTERREICH
Donnerstag, 6. 11. 2008 | diepresse.com | Do 45 / Nr. 18.227 / 1,50 Euro

Die Presse

Telekom vor Verkauf
SP-Spitze trifft TA-Boss Nemsic (Bild): Privatisierung soll Geld in die Staatskasse bringen.
Seite 19, Kommentar S. 35

50 Milliarden Schulden zusätzlich
Staatsschuldenausschuss warnt davor, alle Budget-Dämme brechen zu lassen. Seite 9

★ 11 Seiten zu Obamas historischem Wahlsieg ★

DIE NEUEN VEREINIGTEN STAATEN
Daten, Fakten, Emotionen: Alle Ergebnisse im Detail sowie die große Reportage vom Wahlabend. **Seiten 2, 3**

„DER WAHRE GEIST AMERIKAS"
Im Wortlaut: Barack Obamas Rede nach der Entscheidung vor über 100.000 Menschen. **Seite 34**

68

Ten photos of jubilance, tears, and pumping fists conveyed the emotion of Obama's victory.

Obamas Amerika

CHANGE. Der neue Präsident steht für die Hoffnungen eines veränderten Amerika: jünger, farbiger, weiblicher. Die Erwartungen sind gewaltig.

VON BURKHARD BISCHOF

Nach 43 Präsidenten, die ausnahmslos aus britisch-, irisch- oder deutschstämmigen Familien kamen, hat nun Barack Obama, der Sohn eines kenianischen Austauschstudenten, das beste Ergebnis eines demokratischen Präsidentschaftsbewerbers seit Lyndon B. Johnson 1964 erreicht.

Das kam nicht zuletzt durch eine beispiellose Wählermobilisierung zustande: 66 Prozent der Amerikaner gingen wählen, so viele wie seit 100 Jahren nicht mehr. Und das Gesicht der amerikanischen Mehrheit hat sich in diesem Massenansturm auf die Urnen entscheidend verändert. Beobachter nennen es die „Obama-Koalition": Schwarze, Hispanics, Frauen, Erst- und Jungwähler stimmten mehrheitlich für Obama.

Noch nie gingen so viele Afroamerikaner wählen wie am Dienstag (sie machten 13 Prozent der Wähler aus), und 95 Prozent von ihnen stimmten für Barack Obama. Auch rund zwei Drittel der Wähler mit lateinamerikanischem und karibischem Hintergrund entschieden sich für Obama. Es ist dies die am stärksten wachsende Bevölkerungsgruppe in den Vereinigten Staaten.

56 Prozent der weiblichen Wähler gaben für Obama ihre Stimme ab. Frauen in den USA tendieren bei Wahlen allerdings immer eher zu den Demokraten. Erdrutschartig hingegen das Wahlverhalten der Erst- und Jungwähler: Unter den Erstwählern stimmten fast 70 Prozent für den Demokraten, in der Gruppe der unter 30-Jährigen liegt er um 34 Prozentpunkte vor dem republikanischen Kandidaten John McCain.

Obama konnte mit seinen Botschaften der Veränderung aber auch in den besser gebildeten und wohlhabenderen Schichten punkten, er eroberte mit Florida, Ohio, Pennsylvania, Indiana, Virginia oder New Mexico Bundesstaaten, deren Wähler traditionell zu den Republikanern tendieren.

Eine Kernfrage ist für politische Analytiker nun, wie Obama angesichts seiner Wählerkoalition und der Wahlmotive sein Präsidentschaftsmandat interpretieren wird. War das Wahlergebnis vom Dienstag (52 zu 48 Prozent für Obama) in erster Linie eine Absage an die Bush-Regierung und das Versagen der Republikaner während der vergangenen acht Jahre? Oder war es ein Votum für eine liberale – im europäischen Sinne – sozialdemokratische Politik?

Die Erwartungen, die Obama mit seinen Botschaften quer durch die amerikanische Bevölkerung geweckt hat, sind jedenfalls gewaltig. Umso größer ist die Gefahr eines rasanten Absturzes, wenn Barack Obama nach seinem Amtsantritt am 20. Jänner 2009 nicht rasch und konsequent Taten setzt, die mit den Hoffnungen, die er geweckt hat, im Einklang stehen.

PREISE: Deutschland, Italien, Slowenien € 2,-, Belgien € 2,80, Slowakei € 2,66 (SKK 80), HRK 14, ČZK 65, Ft 390. „DIE PRESSE", 1030 Wien, Hainburger Str. 33, PF 33. ☏ (01) 514 14. Fax: DW 400 (Redaktion); DW 250 (Anzeigen). **ABO:** ☏ (01) 514 14 DW 70, Fax: DW 71. Verlagspostamt: 1030 Wien, P.b.b. Zulassungsnummer: 02Z032748T

NAVIGATOR

Heute mit „Tele"-Fernsehprogramm.
[Fotos: Reuters, Diyait, AP (8), EPA (3), Reuters]

US-Wahl online
Detailergebnisse, Analysen, Reaktionen und Bilder
diepresse.com/us-wahl

DeMorgen

ONAFHANKELIJK DAGBLAD €1

PRESIDENT
OBAMA
Historische
bijlage
12 PAGINA'S
EXTRA

DONDERDAG 6 NOVEMBER 2008 ● WWW.DEMORGEN.BE

FOTO EPA

CHANGE

CHANGEMENT 变化 DEĞIŞIM
PROMĚNA
ÄNDERUNG MUUTTAA
ИЗМЕНЕНИЕ CAMBIO
VERANDER
ENDERUNG تغيير VÁLTOZÁS ZMIANA
BREYTING
CAMBIAMENTO BADILI
SCHIMBARE MENGUBAH MUDANÇA
þanøo VEKSLE 변화
VERANDERING

CHANGE in het Frans, Duits, Chinees, Turks, Tsjechisch, Fins,
Russisch, Spaans, Afrikaans, Jiddisch, Lislands, Arabisch,
Hongaars, Pools, Italiaans, Swahili, Roemeens, Indonesisch,
Portugees, Esperanto, Zweeds, Koreaans, Nederlands

PRIJS: 1 euro ● Nederland en Luxemburg: 1,75 euro ● Hoofdredacteurs: Klaus Van Isacker & Bart Van Doorne ● Uitgave: De Persgroep Publishing ● De Morgen · Arduinkaai 29 · 1000 Brussel ● Abonnementen: 02/454.25.91 ● Advertenties: 02/542.10.10 ● Promotie: 02/454.26.83 ● Redactie: 02/555.68.11 [fax 02/520.35.15] ● e-mail: info@demorgen.be

69

The Flemish-language daily in Brussels captured Obama's victory with a single word, change, translated into two dozen languages.

70

With just a bit more blue than red, the Canadian daily declared "Obama Elected."

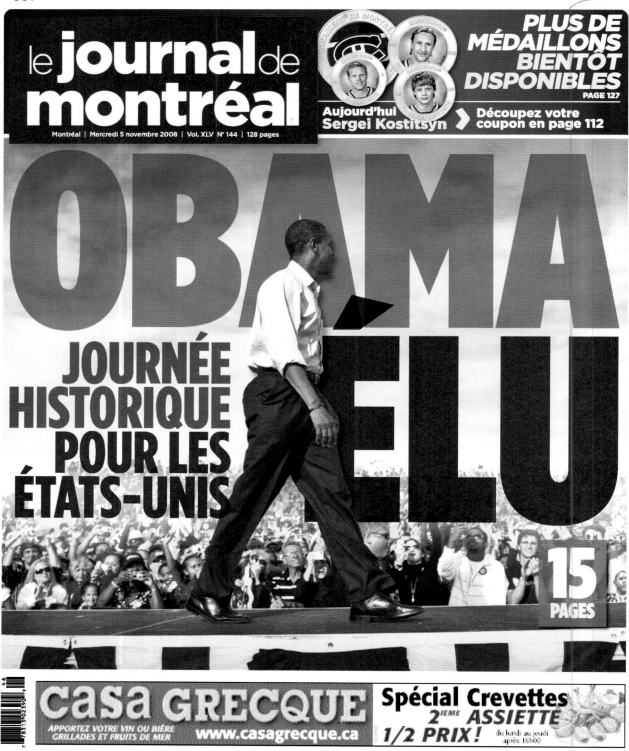

EL COLOMBIANO

7 704354 000015 | $1.200 | Año 97 N° 32.750. 32 páginas en cuatro cuadernillos INTERNET: www.elcolombiano.com CORREO ELECTRÓNICO: elcolombiano@elcolombiano.com.co ISSN 0122-0802 | **Miércoles**

Medellín, 5 de noviembre de 2008

Obama Presidente
Primer negro en llegar a la Casa Blanca

EL SENADOR DEMÓCRATA prometió el cambio y anoche comenzó a escribir una página histórica para Estados Unidos.

Histórico. Estados Unidos vio anoche una nueva luz y eligió al senador Barack Obama como su presidente y, de paso, lo invistió con todos los poderes, pues el Partido Demócrata alcanzó, además, la mayoría en el Senado y se perfilaba como ganador en la Cámara. Obama superó ampliamente los 270 votos electorales que necesitaba para ganar. McCain reconoció sobre las 11:15 de la noche el triunfo de Obama. "E.U. habló y habló claro", dijo.

Obama ganó en estados clave como Ohio, Florida y Pensilvania. **INTERNACIONAL 6A A 9A**

REUTERS

71

The paper portrayed Obama striding across its front page, describing him as "writing a historic page for the United States."

SUMARIO TEMÁTICO

■ Información ■ Tendencias
■ Corectividad ■ Comercial ■ Especiales

Recomendados

El general Montoya dio un paso al lado

Luego de 39 años en las Fuerzas Militares y una carrera cargada de condecoraciones y logros, el general Mario Montoya dejó ayer su mando. Lo remplaza el gral. Óscar González

PAZ Y D.H. 12A

Vacío por una ausencia

El General Montoya fue uno de los abanderados de la Política de Seguridad Democrática. Ojalá siga sirviendo a Colombia en otros campos. Así los violentos y uno que otro político de ambiciones desbordadas no podrán seguir celebrando porque se han sacado del zapato la piedra que les estorbaba. Mientras tanto sentiremos el vacío por su ausencia.

EDITORIAL 5A

✉ 9333@elcolombiano.com.co | ☎ 339 3333 | 📞 9333 | ↖ www.elcolombiano.com/tips

SOUVENIR EDITION

The Daily Telegraph

ELECTION

Thursday, November 6, 2008   No 47,721   **BRITAIN'S BEST-SELLING QUALITY DAILY**

The dream comes true

America's first black President completes an epic journey begun by Martin Luther King

Anne Applebaum

THE maps on the television screens started turning blue as soon as the polls had closed on the East Coast; by midnight, John McCain had conceded the presidency to Barack Obama. But I had known the election result many hours before. I did not have special access to internal campaign data, or an early glimpse of the exit polls. I simply had one conversation, and one email exchange, which together told me everything I needed to know.

The conversation was with my sister, who lives in Florida, a bitterly contested battleground state. Florida was split down the middle in 2000, went for George W Bush in 2004, and was considered a possible McCain state this year. But as election day dawned, my sister told me that even though a huge percentage of Floridians had taken advantage of early voting, there were still queues – everywhere – and many of those standing in them were black. Clearly, those waiting, sometimes for hours, were not waiting to vote for McCain.

The subsequent email exchange was with an old friend, a staunch Republican who is married to an even staunher Republican – a rather famous one too. Despite this family circumstance she had, she confessed, just voted for Mr Obama. Though she had had her doubts, she suddenly found, on election day, that the decision was easy.

More than easy: uplifting. When she emerged from the polling booth, she had a spring in her step, because she had just voted for the first black president. "And that's no small thing," she wrote. "Maybe even worth some higher taxes."

And that was how, by about 10am, East Coast time, before the polls had opened in much of the country, I knew two extremely important pieces of information.

Number one: black Americans were, for the first time in recent history, already voting in high numbers. Really high numbers. If the image of the 2000 election was that of lawyers flocking to Florida to dispute the result, 2008 will be remembered for those first-time voters, patiently waiting their turn to mark a ballot or pull a lever. The Obama campaign had identified and steadily lobbied some 600,000 Florida blacks who registered to vote but did not show up in the past. Their efforts paid off, in Florida and everywhere else.

Number two: not just Democrats, not just independents, not just "swing voters" but actual, hard-core Republicans were so moved by the prospect of a black president – and so disgusted by the Bush administration – that they switched sides and voted for Mr Obama. This happened despite accusations that Mr Obama was a socialist, a Marxist, a secret Muslim, a

radical. None of those epithets really stuck. In the end his inclusive, centrist, bipartisan rhetoric proved more powerful than even the hard evidence of his solid, Left-liberal voting record.

He repeated some of it again in his acceptance speech, after quoting Abraham Lincoln, who was a Republican: "I may not have won your vote tonight," he told Mr McCain's electorate, "but I hear your voices. I want your help and I will be your president too."

As a rule, I dislike the word "historic" when used to describe elections: all elections are "historic", after all. Despite the rhetoric, this election is not "historic" in the sense that it presented the American people with some kind of monumental choice between presidents who would have had vastly different policies.

Let us be clear: whoever walks into the White House on inauguration day has limited choices, narrow possibilities, and almost no room for manoeuvre. Left, Right, Democratic or Republican, it does not matter: the new

president still has to make sure that banks continue to lend money, the housing market continues to function, Afghanistan and Iraq do not deteriorate into chaos. I have no doubt that President McCain would have made many of the same decisions as will President Obama.

Nevertheless, this was a completely different election and it has produced a kind of euphoria that I have never seen in American politics before. "Change" did not seem like much of a slogan, when Obama supporters held it up on signs during rallies. "Yes, We Can" did not seem like much of a clarion call.

But when the first black President-elect took the podium, with the black First Lady in waiting beside him, it was impossible not to feel that something profound really had just changed. If nothing else, the worst chapter of the American story – a chapter that began more than three centuries ago, when the first slave ships docked in Britain's North American colonies – had just come to an end.

Early yesterday, black Americans were sending a text

The moment of truth: America's President-Elect Barack Obama kisses his wife Michelle after his victory speech to a cheering crowd in Chicago yesterday

message to one another: "Rosa sat so Martin could walk. Martin walked so Barack could run. Barack is running so our children can fly." Rosa was Rosa Parks, who refused to give up her seat to a white man on an Alabama bus. Martin was Martin Luther King, who marched on Washington and quoted the Declaration of Independence back at Americans: "We hold these truths to be self-evident, that

all men are created equal." Mr Obama is their inheritor – and he knew it. "If there is anyone out there who still doubts that America is a place where all things are possible," he told a cheering, weeping Chicago crowd; and if anyone "still wonders if the dream of our founders is alive in our time – tonight is your answer".

Mr McCain knew it too. In a gracious concession speech, he praised Mr Obama for "inspiring the hopes of so many millions of Americans who had once wrongly believed that they had little at stake or little influence in the election of an American president".

A century ago, he reminded his audience, President Theodore Roosevelt, was condemned for inviting the black educator Booker T Washington to dinner at the White House. "America today is a world away from the cruel and frightful bigotry of that time. There is no better evidence of this than the election of an African American to the presidency of the United States."

I am convinced it was not, in the end, a disadvantage for Mr Obama to be black. His race

was an enormous attraction for many white Americans, even – or perhaps especially – some white Republicans.

Here is something that may be hard for foreigners to understand: Americans desperately want to believe their country stands for fairness, for equality, for democracy. After the mistakes made in Iraq and Guantanamo, the terrible financial crisis, the embarrassment of Hurricane Katrina, a vote for Mr Obama allowed Americans to believe, once again, that the United States is still a virtuous nation.

It is not just about being liked abroad, though being liked is nice: it is about being certain that we still are, as we have often told ourselves, an example to other nations, a "city on a hill".

Americans stood in line for that certainty, they crossed party lines to vote for it, they donated record amounts of money to the Obama campaign in search of it.

In, the end, it comes down to this: all Americans are told, as children, that "anyone can grow up to be president of the United States." And now, once again, we know that it is true.

PATEK PHILIPPE
GENEVE

Begin your own tradition.

Annual Calendar
Ref. 5146J

G Collins & Sons Limited
76/78 High Street, Royal Tunbridge Wells, Kent, TN1 1YB
Tel: 01892 534018 · Fax: 01892 510536
Email: info@gcollinsandsons.com · www.gcollinsandsons.com

The victory address

❝If there is anyone out there who still doubts that America is a place where all things are possible, who still wonders if the dream of our founders is alive in our time, who still questions the power of our democracy – **tonight is your answer**❞

Inside

72

This British daily often features an editorial cartoon on its front page, and on November 6 the cartoon depicted a fountain in front of the White House with a sign reading, "Please do not walk on the water."

BUSINESS MARKETS FALL AFTER OBAMA BOUNCE B1 | FTSE 100 ▽4530.7 -108.7 | DOW JONES ▽9139.27 -486.01

JAKARTA, INDONESIA

The Jakarta Post

Thursday, November 6, 2008 — TWENTY-FOUR PAGES — Vol. 26 No. 189

Ex-lawmakers admit to receiving BI money

Page 9

Sangeh: Bali's popular monkey forest preserve

Page 16

Garcia aiming for No. 2 ranking

Page 22

BARRY'S DONE IT!

Douglas Birch and Steven R. Hurst
Associated Press/Washington

American voters broke with the nation's history of racial divisions and overwhelmingly elected Barack Obama as the U.S.'s first black president, turning to an inspiring young Democratic senator to lead a country weary from war, economic turmoil and eight years of Republican rule.

Obama, embracing a message of change, tore up the U.S. political map as he defeated John McCain, the veteran Republican senator who struggled in vain to distance himself from George W. Bush's presidency, which had grown as unpopular at home as it is abroad.

The election of Obama, the son of black man from Kenya and a white woman from Kansas, marked a turning point for a nation haunted by a legacy of slavery and legal segregation of the races.

"If there is anyone out there who still doubts that America is a place where all things are possible; who still wonders if the dream of our founders is alive in our time; who still questions the power of our democracy, tonight is your answer," Obama told a crowd of about 240,000 supporters in Chicago's Grant Park.

"Change has come to America," he said.

Preparations for an Obama presidency were already underway Wednesday. With just 76 days until the inauguration, Obama is expected to move quickly to begin assembling a White House staff and selecting Cabinet nominees.

When Obama takes office Jan. 20 as the 44th U.S. president, he may face more difficult challenges both at home and abroad than any new U.S. president since the Great Depression.

But he will do so with many allies in Congress, as his Democratic Party expanded its majorities in both chambers. And he will take office with broad popular support.

He scored a decisive win in the electoral vote, the state-by-state tally that determines the winner.

Obama needed only 270 votes to claim the presidency, but sailed to victory with 349 to McCain's 147, with three states still too close to call. Voter turnout, still being counted, was expected to shatter records.

Obama's supporters cheered, screamed and waved flags, welcoming his election in a delirious victory celebration in his hometown. Many, including civil rights leader and two-time presidential candidate Jesse Jackson, had tears in their eyes.

In cities around the country, drivers honked horns through the night. In New York City's Harlem neighborhood, the roar of thousands of people gathered in a plaza near the legendary Apollo Theater could be heard blocks away.

Obama's victory marked the rise of a new generation of American leadership, after 16 years of presidents who came of age during the Vietnam War era. Obama, 47, was still a child when most U.S. troops came home.

It was also Americans' final, symbolic rejection of Bush's presidency. Bush's popularity soared after the Sept. 11, 2001, terrorist attacks, then collapsed with his administration's bungled response to Hurricane Katrina in 2005, the war in Iraq, and to the regulatory lapses that many think led to the U.S. financial crisis.

The race was the longest, most expensive and most riveting in memory. Both Obama and McCain had been on the campaign train for almost two years.

McCain called his former rival to concede defeat - and mark the end of his own 10-year quest for the White House. "The American people have spoken, and spoken clearly," McCain told disappointed supporters in Arizona.

"This is an historic election, and I recognize the special significance it has for African-Americans and the special pride that must be theirs tonight," he said. "These are difficult times for our country. And I pledge to him tonight to do all in my power to help him lead us through the many challenges we face."

Bush added his congratulations from the White House and promised a smooth transition. "What an awesome night for you," he told Obama shortly after the race was decided.

An Obama presidency offers the prospect of a new style and tone in American foreign policy.

Obama has said he will try to withdraw U.S. troops from Iraq in 16 months and has called for a new opening to U.S. adversaries, such as Iran and Cuba. He has urged the closing of the Guantanamo Bay prison and favors cap-and-trade systems to reduce global warming.

Internationally, Obama is hugely popular — a sharp contrast to Bush. Part of his appeal is his personal story that highlights American multiculturalism: Besides his Kenyan father, he has a half-sister who is the daughter of an Indonesian.

In his campaign, Obama mined a deep vein of national discontent, promising Americans hope and change throughout a nearly flawless 21-month campaign for the White House.

He first soared into the national spotlight with his electrifying speech at the 2004 Democratic National Convention, when he made his first run for the Senate. He offered a message of unity to a country mired in partisan anger.

More stories on Pages 3, 11,12

Reuters/John Gress

DEFINING MOMENT: U.S. president-elect Barack Obama *(right)* hugs his wife Michelle as U.S. vice president-elect Joe Biden embraces his wife Jill on stage during their election night party before 240,000 electrified supporters in Chicago's Grant Park on Tuesday (Wednesday morning in Jakarta).

JP/J. Adiguna

PRODIGAL SON: Students of state primary school SDN Menteng 01 in Central Jakarta, where Barack Obama studied during his brief stay in Indonesia in the late-1960s, cheer the U.S. president-elect after learning Wednesday of his victory in Tuesday's historic vote.

Jakarta celebrates the Menteng Kid's victory

The Jakarta Post
Jakarta

Jakarta shared the anxiety and the joy of the U.S presidential election won by new Indonesian darling Barack Hussein Obama on Wednesday.

It was a special day for students of Obama's former school SDN Menteng 01, Central Jakarta, who gathered at the school's hall to watch the final results pour in. Several pictures of Obama during his school years there were prominently displayed.

A 15-minute silence has been held here every day since Monday to allow the students to pray for Obama's victory.

"Every day we have something different to pray for, but since Monday we have prayed for him," said principal Kuwadiyanto.

Obama, or Barry as he was affectionately called during his time in Indonesia, enrolled in the school — then named SD Besuki — as a third-grader in 1968. He previously attended the Fransiskus Asisi Catholic School, also in Central Jakarta.

Obama's historic election as the next U.S. president was a dream come true for his supporters in Indonesia.

"I think it's good motivation for the children to study hard and set their dreams high," Kuwadiyanto said.

Israella Dharmawan, Barry's former teacher at Fransiskus Asisi and an avid follower of the U.S. election, said she was proud and touched by Barry's win.

"I hope to see him become a good president and keep his campaign promises," she said, adding he was good, cheerful and easygoing as a young boy.

"I remember he once wrote two stories titled 'My mother, my idol' and 'I want to be a president'," she said.

Obama's former classmates at SDN Menteng 01 also recalled the times they spent at Café Pisa, Menteng, with the now U.S. president-elect.

Obama moved to Indonesia at the age of six with his mother Ann Dunham and his Indonesian stepfather Lolo Soetoro. He lived in Jakarta from 1967 to 1971.

In the rest of the capital, Jakartans cheered the election of *Anak Menteng* (the Menteng Kid) as America's first black president.

"Though I am not an American, I am very happy to hear that a child who studied in Menteng will be the next U.S. president," Sugiyono, a taxi driver, said after hearing radio reports of Obama's win.

The U.S. Embassy and USINDO organized a U.S. Election Day event at the InterContinental Hotel's Grand Ballroom. Most of the guests were non-Americans.

"It's no longer a U.S. election," one guest said. "It looks like an international election. People all over the world are eagerly awaiting the outcome of the election."

Among U.S. Ambassador Cameron R. Hume's invited guests were presidential spokesmen Dino Patti Djalal and Andi Mallarangeng, former ministers Emil Salim and Alwi Shihab, members of the House of Representatives, scholars, journalists and diplomats.

Despite their busy schedules, the British, Swiss, German, Austrian, Brazilian, Mexican, Jordanian, Tunisian, Palestinian and Singaporean ambassadors turned up to witness the historic moment.

Enda Nasution, who chairs the Obama for Indonesia society, celebrated Obama's victory with 300 members of the group, which was founded over the Internet.

"It's great to be part of history. No one thought Obama would win the U.S. presidency," Enda said.

Mulyani's bosses annul Bakrie suspension lift

Aditya Suharmoko and Rendi A. Witular
The Jakarta Post/Jakarta

The government annulled a decision Wednesday by the Indonesia Stock Exchange (IDX) to lift a trading suspension on PT Bumi Resources, in a move experts say is aimed at keeping the interests of the influential Bakrie family intact.

Before morning trading, the IDX said in a statement it would lift the Bumi suspension after hearing PT Bakrie & Brothers' explanation about a deal to sell its 35 percent stake in Bumi to Northstar Pacific.

The decision was believed to be supported by Finance Minister Sri Mulyani Indrawati, whose ministry oversees the Capital Market Supervisory and Financial Institutions Agency (Bapepam-LK).

However, the IDX scrapped its decision an hour later after a request from the government.

"After considering a request from the government, the exchange decided to delay lifting the suspension until further notice," the IDX said in a statement.

IDX president director Erry Firmansyah refused to explain the reason behind the request.

"It's the government who wanted it, the government of the Republic of Indonesia," he said, refusing to identify which institution had demanded the suspension.

A source at the Finance Ministry said the request was not from the ministry, and Mulyani did not comment on the issue.

"It was a request from an office higher than that run by Mulyani," the source said.

Presidential spokesman Andi Mallarangeng dismissed speculation President Susilo Bambang Yudhoyono was behind the intervention, saying the Bakrie mess was not the President's concern.

Capital market analyst Yanuar Rizky said the government's shocking intercession had diluted its own credibility as the referee of the capital market.

"This move proves there are conflicts of interest among factions within the government to protect certain ruling elites," he said.

Trading in shares of Bakrie & Brothers, Bumi and PT Energi Mega Persada — all part of the Bakrie Group of companies — have been suspended by the IDX since Oct. 7, following sharp falls in share prices due to reports Bakrie was having trouble with debt repayments.

Bakrie & Brothers, the nation's largest publicly listed investment firm, announced on Nov. 1 that Northstar, a local unit of U.S. buyout giant Texas Pacific Group, had agreed to pay US$1.3 billion for its 35 percent stake in Bumi.

Northstar, believed to be teaming up with state mining firms, must wrap up the deal within 28 days.

Analysts say a lifting of the suspension would have harmed the deal, with the Bumi stake expected to be heavily devaluated as investors promptly sell them over worries the stake could drop further due to uncertainties over Bakrie's debt arrangements.

Help from the government will mean a lot for the Bakrie family, headed by Coordinating Minister for the People's Welfare Aburizal Bakrie, following its role as a key financier of Yudhoyono's 2004 presidential campaign. **(hwa)**

San Miguel — Page 13

Referring to Obama by his childhood nickname, the Indonesian paper reported from the school he attended as a third-grader in Jakarta.

www.israelhayom.co.il

30	32	36	37	40
כלכלה היום סנדיסק צפויה לפטר מאה עובדים בארץ	**דעות היום** דן מרגלית על ניצחון אובאמה, בגין ופרידמן	**קוראים היום** קריסתה של האהבה מבלי להגיע לגאולה	**לאן היום** מכון ויצמן וחגיגה רומנית ברחובות	**ספורט היום** הערב: מכבי ת"א מול לה מאן ביורוליג

★ **הבוקר שאחרי: אמריקה והעולם מתעוררים למציאות חדשה** ★

עידן אובאמה

ניצחון מתוק

רגע אינטימי של נחת בין בני הזוג אובאמה, לעיני מאות אלפי תומכים מריעים

גיליון מיוחד

אמריקה מסתכלת בראי ולראשונה זה זמן רב – מרוצה מעצמה ● לאחר האופוריה מתחילה העבודה הקשה ● הבוקר יקבל הנשיא הנבחר את התדריך הראשון מראש הסי.איי.אי ● וול־סטריט נתנה לאובאמה כתף קרה: ירדה ב־5% ● ובפתח: המשבר הכלכלי, איראן והמזרח התיכון ● בועז ביסמוט, וושינגטון, עמ' 02-25

הקשר הישראלי של ראש הצוות

רם עמנואל, בן לישראלי לשעבר, יהיה ראש צוות הבית הלבן ● בימי מלחמת המפרץ הראשונה התנדב לשירות אזרחי בצה"ל ● עמ' 05

דיויד פרום
סיבה לדאגה

לישראל יש סיבה לדאגה. בעבר היה לה נוח עם נשיאים אמריצינגליים כמו קלינטון, או נשיאים שהכינו את חשיבות הקשר כמו ניקסון. אבל לאובאמה אין קשר רגשי לי־שראל וגם לא הבנה בעניני חוץ. עמ' 09

פרופ' אברהם בן־צבי
הפכה עורה

קואליציית ענק חדשה, חוצת גבולות של צבע, דת ומעמד – זה מה שברק אובא־מה הצליח לבנות סביבו. מעתה יהיו שם גם בני המעמד הבינוני־גבוה, אנשי ההיי־טק ואנשי העסקים, והצעירים. עמ' 24

דוד ויצטום
מקרין את הדימוי

אובאמה לקח על אחד את דמות הנשיא השחור מהסדרה "24" ואימץ אותה, עם המנהיגות, הרטוריקה וההלי־כה על הבמה. הוא מקרין את הדימוי שהוא רוצה למכור לציבור. עמ' 23

חמי שלו
תקוות גדולות

המצביעים בארה"ב חוללו רעידת אדמה, שאת גלי ההרף שלה נחוש כו־לנו עוד שנים ארוכות. זה לא מהפך – זו מהפכה, ולא רק שריקת סיום החלטית לתקופתו של ג'ורג' בוש. עמ' 02

---

50 קסאמים ופצמ"רים נורו ליישובי הנגב ולאשקלון עמ' 26-27

היום דיון שרונים בעבודה; פואד במקום שישי מתי טוכפלד, עמ' 28

» עוד מהמחשה: העילוונה התהווה אניתם הושלכו על משת"פים « שלומי דיאז עמ' 27

Japan's Asahi Shimbun *declared that U.S. Democrats were back in power, thanks to a new president who had "grown up in Hawaii and Indonesia."*

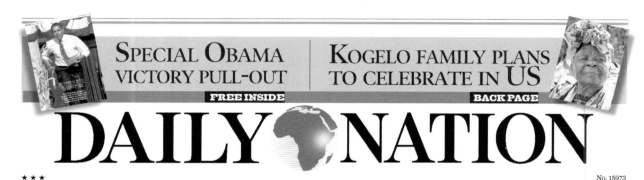

SPECIAL OBAMA VICTORY PULL-OUT
FREE INSIDE

KOGELO FAMILY PLANS TO CELEBRATE IN US
BACK PAGE

DAILY NATION

★ ★ ★

No. 15973

www.nation.co.ke   NAIROBI, THURSDAY, NOVEMBER 6, 2008   KSh35/00 (TSh800/00 : UShl,500/00)

76

Obama's Kenyan roots helped drive sales of this edition from its usual press run of 190,000 copies up to 300,000.

NEW DAWN IN AMERICA

THE FIRST FAMILY

How Obama won by a landslide

SPECIAL REPORTS: Pages 2-9, 13-20

NEWS 2-9, BACK | OPINION 10-11 | SPECIAL REPORT 13-20 | INTERNATIONAL 23-28 | BUSINESS 30-33 | SPORT 67-71

CZWARTEK
6 listopada 2008
NR 260. 5870
NAKŁAD 432 TYS. 3
1,50 zł
w tym 7% VAT

REDAKTOR PROWADZĄCY
ZBIGNIEW PENDEL
WYDAJE AGORA SA
NUMER INDEKSU

www.wyborcza.pl

REKLAMA
Hity dnia
w telewizji nowej generacji n:
str.25
HDTV

OBAMERYKA!

40 lat temu, gdy biały zamachowiec zabił Martina Luthera Kinga, byłam w brzuchu mamy. Strasznie się bała, wybuchały zamieszki. A teraz... Barack Obama, Murzyn, prezydentem! Ledwie 40 lat!

MARCIN BOSACKI, CHICAGO

- Nie mogę uwierzyć, nie mogę w to uwierzyć! O Boże, Boże wszechmogący!!! - krzyczała stojąca obok mnie Micheline Head, 40-letnia Murzynka z zachodniego Chicago, gdy na wielkim telebimie ogłoszono, że Barack Obama, 47-letni senator z Illinois, zostanie 44. prezydentem USA.

Staliśmy w dwustutysięcznym tłumie w parku Granta w Chicago, obok nas ludzie krzyczeli, machali flagami, rzucali się sobie w objęcia.

- Dziś cały dzień się modliłam, a dziś dzień się trzęsłam, nie wierzyłam, że to się może stać, a jednak! Widzi pan, 40 lat temu, gdy biały zamachowiec zabił Martina Luthera Kinga, byłam w brzuchu mamy. W całym kraju wybuchały zamieszki, mama strasznie się bała. A teraz... Obama, Murzyn, prezydentem! Ledwie 40 lat! - ekscytowała się Micheline.

W tym momencie zaczęła płakać. Kiedy się ciut uspokoiła, wyszeptała: - To jest Ameryka... To jest Ameryka.

Gdy Obama zaczął przemawiać nad ranem czasu polskiego, Micheline z tysiącami ludzi zaczęła krzyczeć główne hasło jego kampanii: „Yes, we can!" (Tak, damy radę!).

Nowy prezydent USA, który zostanie zaprzysiężony 20 stycznia, mówił: - Jeśli ktoś wciąż wątpi, czy Ameryka jest miejscem, w którym wszystko jest

możliwe, jeśli ktoś kwestionuje żywotność naszej demokracji, to dziś otrzymał odpowiedź! To odpowiedź udzielona przez młodych i starych, bogatych i biednych, demokratów i republikanów, czarnych, białych, Latynosów, Azjatów i rdzennych mieszkańców tej ziemi, homo- i heteroseksualistów, niepełnosprawnych i zdrowych. Słowem - Amerykanów, którzy wysłali w świat przesłanie, że nigdy nie byliśmy tylko zlepkiem stanów republikańskich i stanów demokratycznych. Jesteśmy i zawsze będziemy Stanami Zjednoczonymi Ameryki!

Gdy Obama skupiony, może nawet spięty, mówił, że „do Ameryki nadeszła zmiana", wielu ludzi płakało. Ten młody polityk, cztery lata temu zupełnie nieznany Ameryce, nie dość, że został pierwszym Afroamerykaninem, który wygrał wybory prezydenckie, to jeszcze zrobił to bardzo zdecydowanie - pokonał republikanina Johna McCaina 53 do 46 proc. W liczbie elektorów, którzy formalnie wybiorą prezydenta USA, jego przewaga jest ogromna - demokrata zdobył prawdopodobnie 364 głosy, republikanin - 174 (wczoraj liczono jesz-

cze głosy w dwóch stanach). Obama zwyciężył w kilku bardzo konserwatywnych stanach, gdzie demokrata nie wygrał od 40 lat.

Obama pokonał McCaina, bo potrafił przekonać wyborców, że lepiej poradzi sobie z kryzysem gospodarczym. Gospodarka była głównym kryterium dla prawie dwóch trzecich Amerykanów, walka z terrorem i wojna w Iraku - tylko dla mniej więcej 10 proc. Dla ponad połowy wyborców bardzo ważne było „zerwanie z polityką Busha" - głosowali na demokratę.

Co dla Ameryki może najważniejsze, rasa Obamy nie grała negatywnej roli. Dostał głosy 43 proc. białych wyborców - więcej wśród demokratów miał tylko Jimmy Carter w 1976 r., tyle samo Bill Clinton w 1992 r. Wśród białych wyborców wygrał jednak McCain. Ale Obama dostał aż 95 proc. głosów Afroamerykanów i 66 proc. Latynosów.

Co prawda 20 proc. głosujących stwierdziło, że rasa była dla nich ważna, ale większość z nich - i czarnych, i białych - widziała w niej atut Obamy.

W mowie zwycięstwa Obama mówił o 106-letniej Ann Nixon Cooper, która głosowała w Atlancie. - Gdy Ann się rodziła, nie mogła głosować z dwóch powodów - bo była kobietą i była czarnoskóra. Na tym polega prawdziwy geniusz Ameryki - że Ameryka potrafi się zmieniać.

Gdy Obama to mówił, Micheline znów płakała. I mówiła cicho: - To jest Ameryka. To jest Ameryka. ◉

SONDAŻ „GAZETY": POLACY ZA OBAMĄ

Czy cieszysz się, że Barack Obama wygrał wybory prezydenckie w USA?		Czy Barack Obama będzie lepszym, czy gorszym prezydentem niż Bush dla...		Czy to dobrze, czy źle, że prezydentem światowego mocarstwa został...	
Tak	**52** proc.	...USA:		...polityk, który chce zerwać z polityką Busha:	
Nie	**14** proc.	**Lepszym**	**73** proc	**Dobrze**	**73** proc
		Gorszym	**7** proc.	**Źle**	**11** proc.
		...Europy:		...człowiek stosunkowo młody:	
		Lepszym	**60** proc.	**Dobrze**	**87** proc.
		Gorszym	**15** proc.	**Źle**	**9** proc.
		...Polski:		...polityk ciemnoskóry:	
		Lepszym	**54** proc.	**Dobrze**	**70** proc.
		Gorszym	**20** proc.	**Źle**	**11** proc.

PBS DGA dla „Gazety", 5 listopada, badanie telefoniczne, próba reprezentatywna 500 osób. Pominięto odpowiedzi „trudno powiedzieć"

ALBUM W SPRZEDAŻY
ODZYSKIWANIE NIEPODLEGŁEJ
1918

77

Gazeta Wyborcza, the Polish daily born of the Solidarity movement (the paper's name means "Election Gazette"), coined a word in Polish to sum up the new American landscape.

Público

www.publico.es | AÑO II - Nº405 | JUEVES 6 DE NOVIEMBRE DE 2008

EDICIÓN NACIONAL | 50 CÉNTIMOS

78

The Spanish–language paper, which was launched in September 2007, captured Obama's victory with a headline that reflected the change Obama said he would bring as president.

OBAMA, **PRESIDENTE**

→ 2 a 14

ARRANCA EL CAMBIO

El demócrata nombra jefe de Gabinete a Rahm Emanuel y encarga a una troika preparar la transición

Gran expectación en todo el mundo ante los primeros pasos del ganador de las elecciones en EEUU

Parlamento PÁGS. 20 Y 21

Las enmiendas del PP hinchan el presupuesto en 650 millones

CIS PÁG. 22

Chacón supera a De la Vega como ministra más valorada

Literatura PÁGS. 40 Y 41

Muere Michael Crichton, autor de 'Parque Jurásico'

Industria PÁG. 30

Barcelona acoge la primera gran manifestación a favor del empleo

CONGRATULATIONS

These journalism associations congratulate all whose work is featured in this collection.

National Press Photographers Association
http://www.nppa.org

American Society of Journalists and Authors
http://www.asja.org

American Society of Newspaper Editors
http://www.asne.org

The Society for News Design
http://www.snd.org

Associated Press Managing Editors
http://www.apme.com

ABOUT THE POYNTER INSTITUTE

The Poynter Institute is a school dedicated to teaching and inspiring journalists and media leaders. Through its seminars, publications, and Web site (http://www.poynter.org), the Institute promotes excellence and integrity in the practice of craft and in the practical leadership of successful businesses. Poynter stands for a journalism that informs citizens, enlightens public discourse, and strengthens the ties between journalism and democracy.

The school offers training at its Florida campus throughout the year in the areas of online and multimedia, leadership and management, reporting, writing, and editing, TV and radio, ethics and diversity, journalism education, and visual journalism. Poynter's e-learning portal, News University (http://www.newsu.org), offers newsroom training to journalists, journalism students, and educators through faculty-led, online seminars, Webinars, and over eighty self-directed courses. Most of these courses are free or low cost and are open to the public.

The Institute was founded in 1975 by Nelson Poynter, chairman of the *St. Petersburg Times* and its Washington affiliate, *Congressional Quarterly*. Before his death, Mr. Poynter willed controlling stock in his companies to the school. As a financially independent, nonprofit organization, The Poynter Institute is beholden to no interest except its own mission: to help journalists seek and achieve excellence.

Sandy Johnakin took tremendous responsibility for the success of this project, managing the permissions and files, staying until all hours, with a smile and laugh throughout. We can't thank her enough.

And finally, Sara Quinn, who coedited this book, reviewed hundreds—possibly thousands—of front pages searching for notable ones, moderated endless debates over which papers to include, helped craft creative captions, and tracked down the dangling details, all while teaching a weeklong seminar, hosting houseguests, and being the colleague you always hope for as a partner. This book would not have been the same without her.

Julie Moos
Editor, Poynter Publications and Poynter Online
The Poynter Institute

ACKNOWLEDGMENTS

Our first and largest debt is to the journalists whose work appears in this book, and the news organizations that employ them and gave us permission to reprint their front pages royalty-free. The pages appear as they were provided to us by newspapers, except for the *Orlando Sentinel*, which was cropped to fit this format and to emphasize the photography it featured.

Unfortunately, we had to limit the number of newspapers we could include. The selection process required balancing page design, geographic diversity, historical importance, and other factors. We left out entire states, even though they were home to some outstanding front pages. Fortunately, you can view all the front pages submitted to us at http://www.poynter.org/electionfrontpages.

We are grateful to The Associated Press for permission to reprint at no cost its photos and stories that appear on the front pages included here.

For research, we relied on various news sources, the participating newspapers, especially *The New York Times*, *Editor & Publisher*, The Pew Research Center, and Wikipedia.

G. B. Trudeau wrote an introduction to this collection that left us dancing in the streets.

At Andrews McMeel Publishing, we thank John McMeel, a gracious and persistent envoy, and Chris Schillig, who is smart, warm, and endlessly patient. We also thank Julie Barnes, Holly Camerlinck, John Carroll, Ren-Whei Harn, Cliff Koehler, Tim Lynch, and David Shaw.

For translations, we depended on Maria Ignacia Errazuriz, Nico Guerrero, Maria Jaimes, Mohsen Milani, Kathleen Mitchell, Grzegorz Piechota, Kiichiro Sato, and Rabbi Michael Torop.

We turned constantly to our Poynter friends and family for help, especially securing permissions, tracking down files, writing captions, coordinating orders, bulk sales, shipping, marketing, partnership relations, and more. For all they've done, we thank Ellyn Angelotti, Alex Bordens, Darla Cameron, Cathy Campbell, Roy Peter Clark, Karen Dunlap, Rick Edmonds, Chrissy Estrada, Howard Finberg, Jill Geisler, Marty Gregor, Nico Guerrero, Tom Huang, Kenny Irby, Maria Jaimes, Gary Moos, Jessica Sandler, Monique Saunders, Chip Scanlan, David Shedden, Jim Stem, Mallary Tenore, Wendy Wallace, Butch Ward, Latishia Williams, Meghan Willoughby, and Keith Woods.

Several colleagues played particularly critical roles. David Shedden's exhibit of front pages in our library and online are a daily inspiration. Bill Mitchell's contacts and collegiality saved us many times. Becky Bowers is such a thorough copy editor, she probably double-checked the spelling of her own name. Steve Myers rechecked it while also lending his excellent writing and reporting skills to this enterprise.